THE WITHERED ARM

Travels over the SR lines West of Exeter 1958-62

Beattie well tank No 30586 on station pilot duties at Wadebridge in the summer of 1959.

From a pencil drawing by the author.

All photographs taken by Peter Barnfield, all artwork created by and © Peter Barnfield.
Designed by Stephen Dent
Printed by Amadeus Press, Cleckheaton

Published by Wild Swan Books Ltd. 3A Upper Lambridge Street, Larkhall, Bath, BA1 6RY
All authors royalties from sales of the book are been donated to Lynton & Barnstaple Railway Project.

Drummond T9 30718 waits in the platform at Padstow in August 1960 with a train for Wadebridge. The state of the lower part of the locomotive's smokebox door leaves a little to be desired in terms of presentation!

... the long express from Waterloo
That takes us down to Cornwall. Tea-time shows
The small fields waiting, every blackthorn hedge
Straining inland before the south-west gale.
The emptying train, wind in the ventilators,
Puffs out of Egloskerry to Tresmeer
Through minty meadows, under bearded trees
And hills upon whose sides the clinging farms
Hold Bible Christians. Can it really be
That this same carriage came from Waterloo?
On Wadebridge station what a breath of sea
Scented the Camel Valley! Cornish air,
Soft Cornish rains, and silence after steam ...

John Betjeman, Summoned by Bells

CONTENTS

INTRODUCTION 4

1 PLYMOUTH FRIARY IN THE RAIN 7
June 1958

2 TO ILFRACOMBE EVENTUALLY 10
A Saturday in June 1959

3 PILGRIMAGE TO WADEBRIDGE 18
Tuesday 18th August 1959

4 The DARTMOOR LINE 25
August 1959

5 TAW & TORRIDGE 37
June 1960

6 WAITING AT HALWILL JUNCTION 46
Saturday 20th August 1960

7 T9s ON THE ATLANTIC COAST 54
Monday 22nd August 1960

8 WITH THE GOODS TO WENFORD 62
Tuesday 14th August 1962

9 MIXED TRAIN TO CALLINGTON 71
Saturday 18th August 1962

10 BREAKFAST AT BUDE 83
Monday 20th August 1962

POSTSCRIPT 92

INTRODUCTION

This is not a detailed railway history, nor is it a list of train times, mileages and engine numbers. It is simply an attempt to record my impressions of journeys over the Southern Region lines to the west of Exeter between the years 1958 and 1962, in the days before British Railways Western Region took control of them and began the systematic dismantling of the system.

At the time I kept a travel diary and it is around the contents of the yellowing pages of this book, lying in a drawer and rediscovered many years later, that these words are written. They are unashamedly nostalgic, but hopefully convey some of the Withered Arm's special atmosphere, an atmosphere which had seen so little change for many years but which was soon to be swept away for ever in the name of progress.

The Withered Arm

Was it that British habit of often backing the underdog that in 1958 aroused my interest in that seemingly almost forgotten Southern system to the west of Exeter? The straggling lines, crossing remote and lightly populated parts of Devon and Cornwall, reaching out for distant outposts, were indeed in some cases not unlike the withered arm of a great, otherwise healthy tree.

But here were all the essential ingredients of a railway lover's pie, bucolic branch trains shuffling slowly along, named expresses thundering down from the moor, mixed trains ambling away the day.

Here in this land of Arthurian Legend, was the grandeur of Dartmoor, the secrecy of wooded valleys and sheltered harbours. Here the thrill of seaside holidays, immortalised by John Betjeman and the untamed Atlantic coast so tellingly portrayed by Thomas Hardy in his novel "A Pair of Blue Eyes". Here also were isolated signalboxes, secluded stations, remote junctions and lonely lines quietly rusting between occasional trains.

To the south, former Great Western main lines echoed to those strange sounds from

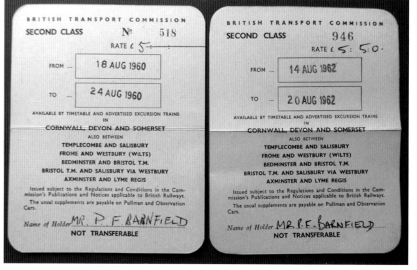

The West of England Railrover tickets that made possible a number of the journeys described in this book at a budget price.

This 1961 view at Luckett station, on the Callington branch, with a rather murky Dartmoor background and plenty of sheep, epitomises the sparsely populated countryside through which many of the Southern's Withered Arm routes ran.

Swindon's diesel hydraulics – for me, they held little if any attraction. The Western Region was firmly in the grip of so called modernisation fervour and putting aside the chocolate and cream W.R. timetable I reached for its much larger, green companion. The section to be scrutinised took up a miniscule portion of its thickness but here were many fascinating places served by a rail system worked entirely by steam locomotives, some of which were undoubtedly museum pieces.

Thumbing through those tissue-thin pages I discovered that one could apparently spend hours, slowly going almost nowhere. Promptly producing paper and pencil I began working out some journeys – they were to prove unforgettable.

	Tuesday 14th August 1962	
dep.	Bristol T.M.	1.55am
arr.	Plymouth	5.15
dep.	Plymouth	6.10
arr.	Liskeard	6.57
dep.	Liskeard	7.25
arr.	Bodmin Road	7.43
dep.	Bodmin Road	7.50
arr.	Wadebridge	8.27
dep.	Wadebridge(goods)	9.30
arr.	Wenfordbridge	12.30
dep.	Wenfordbridge	1.30
arr.	Dunmere	2.45
dep.	Dunmere Halt	3.25
arr.	Bodmin North	3.30
dep.	Bodmin General	3.53
arr.	Bodmin Road	4.01
dep.	Bodmin Road	4.08
arr.	Bristol T.M.	9.35

	Monday 20th August 1962	
dep.	Bristol T.M.	1.55am
arr.	Exeter St. Davids	3.38
dep.	Exeter Central	5.10
arr.	Okehampton	5.57
dep.	Okehampton	6.30
arr.	Halwill Junction	6.58
dep.	Halwill Junction	7.15
arr.	Bude	7.49
dep.	Bude	9.30
arr.	Halwill Junction	10.10
dep.	Halwill Junction	10.38
arr.	Torrington	12.02
dep.	Torrington	12.13
To Exeter, after visit to Seaton branch		
dep.	Exeter St. Davids	6.01
Change at Taunton		
dep.	Taunton	6.50
arr.	Bristol T.M.	8.34

The original tablet was re-engraved 'Port Isaac Road' at some time. What it was originally, we have been unable to find!

1

PLYMOUTH FRIARY
IN THE RAIN

June 1958

My father's 1936 Morris 8 had successfully negotiated the perils of a summer Saturday on the A38, including endless jams on the dreaded Exeter Bypass, and we had arrived at our holiday hotel in Torquay utterly exhausted. In previous years we would have travelled by train of course, but like many thousands of others we had been successfully converted to the joys of gridlock, all the time pretending to ourselves that this was so much more convenient than public transport. I immediately sought refuge at the railway station as an antidote to hours in the back of what was not the most comfortable of cars.

As I approached the station my attention was immediately captured by one of those simple single colour railway posters that festooned platform notice boards in those days and were, in my opinion, far more effective than many of today's multi-coloured leaflets. "Cheap day tickets to Plymouth" proclaimed this particular poster. I'm not sure how much it actually was then, but Plymouth was way beyond pocket money range from my home in Bristol, so the very next day I was back at the station with my government surplus haversack, packed lunch and camera, undaunted by the typical summer holiday rain that was falling steadily.

After a change at Newton Abbot a double-headed express took me over the very damp South Devon banks, through the edge of a Dartmoor mist, down over the old Lee Moor Tramway track and past the massed engines at Laira shed. Now although mid-week North Road station was nowhere near as busy as Bristol Temple Meads, there were completely different sights to see, such as the GW pannier tanks on Saltash auto trains and some of those WR named trains which had previously been mere features in a book or timetable. There was the *Royal Duchy* with immaculate chocolate and cream carriage stock and an equally immaculate Castle class locomotive. Then there was the *Cornish Riviera Express*, also with chocolate and cream stock and hauled by what for me was a very strange creature, D604 the North British built diesel named *Ark Royal*. Well, I expect the actual ship of that name was even then not far away at Devonport, so it was perhaps appropriate motive power for this train as far as Plymouth at any rate, not that I much liked the look of the thing!

This was not why I had come to Plymouth of course as the real attraction for me was the presence of occasional Southern trains which passed through North Road on their way to their terminus at Friary. These were so very different from my staple diet of Swindon copper and brass and besides which there was also something about the name Friary that appealed to the romantic side of my nature. I suppose this was the beginning of my fascination with the Withered Arm even if I didn't quite realise it at the time.

Whatever the reason, some unknown force seemed to compel me to march to the booking office and demand a return ticket to Plymouth Friary. The booking clerk looked somewhat amused at what to me was a perfectly straightforward request. This was apparently quite out of the question and he explained that only single tickets were available. I expected him to suggest my travelling there and back on a city bus, but he presumably took pity on me and sold me a sixpenny single.

So one could travel to Friary but not come back again it seemed. The mystery deepened; what actually happened at this mystery station? Would I be whisked away by cunning monks to a life of servitude in cells beneath the tracks? My youthful imagination worked overtime as, clutching my precious pasteboard single, I misread the number on the departure board and waited in blissful ignorance on completely the wrong side of the station.

The arrival from the Bere Alston direction of a bustling little Adams 02 with two faded maroon examples of L&SWR gated carriages in the platform opposite roused me from my reverie. It took but a moment for the penny to drop before I was off, diving down the subway and leaping up the stairs to the other platform three at a time. 'Right away' had been given on the otherwise deserted platform and the little 0-4-4T had already jerked into motion as I topped the steps. Fortunately the guard saw me sprinting, swung open one of the gates and with a mighty leap … I landed safely in the vestibule beside him. He asked if I had a ticket, and was maybe keen to issue one if indeed he carried such items, but I waved my hard won single and settled into the otherwise empty saloon.

These gated carriages were former trailer cars built by Dugald Drummond to run with his small 'motor tanks', successors to the older 'rail motors' where the loco and carriage were combined as one unit. The trailers were open saloons entered by a

central vestibule which had waist-high, metalwork gates instead of conventional doors. In 1958 these were about 50 years old and nearing the end of their lives.

And thanks were due to the man who designed them, for I would certainly have missed a conventional train. That this venerable combination was still pottering around selective parts of South Devon in 1958 was just one very good reason to be interested in the Southern and the Withered Arm, although I certainly didn't know it by that name in those far off days.

So here we were, after a circuit of Plymouth, rattling into Friary in the rain; I was the only passenger and there was no-one to meet the train. It was damp, everything was grey and dripping and the 02, shrouded in steam, reversed and disappeared somewhere leaving me alone in the steady downpour. Waterloo seemed a very long way away.

Friary station had originally opened for passengers in 1891 and it seemed to me to be much better situated for the older part of Plymouth, such as the Barbican area, than the North Road station. It was 234 miles from Waterloo and there were two main platforms, each sporting a shorter bay on its outer edge. The one time footbridge had by now disappeared, access to the other platform being around the buffer stops and although this was supposedly all under cover, the canopy was anything but watertight.

Stowing my camera in the driest possible place I trudged off the end of the platform, past the signal box and roamed in the rain. The downpour and gloom, although being unpleasant, undoubtedly aided my trespassing as it would probably have been assumed I was a railwayman, had there been anyone actually looking. I discovered a

clutch of 'Woolworths' moguls at the ashy three road engine shed up the line and three of the diminutive B4 0-4-0 tanks. Eventually however the torrents sent me scuttling back to seek such shelter as there was beneath those leaking awnings, where paint peeled and damp coated the cold greystone walls of a once imposing station now in very run down condition.

A train materialised in the departure platform – three coaches whose window stickers proudly proclaimed 'Waterloo', and unrebuilt Bulleid pacific *Hawkinge*, cloaked in leaking steam. Such were the extremely gloomy conditions that I knew photography, with my inexpensive and decidedly substandard camera, was sadly out of the question, and so there would be no photographic record of my visit that day. I kept the camera dry, hoped for better weather later in the week, and elected to ride on this train back round to North Road.

Now came the business of finding someone to issue another single ticket. Knocks on the shuttered booking office window produced no response, investigation of various doors, rooms and dark corners proved completely fruitless. I was just beginning to assume that maybe no-one *could* depart from Friary station, legally at least, when I unearthed a booking clerk in a little room with a teapot; he seemed most surprised to see anyone.

To show his displeasure at having his teabreak disturbed for such a minimal fare, he defaced my sixpenny single ticket with his ball-point pen, a writing instrument which I have always disliked intensely. The fare had been five pence but by now it was obviously not thought necessary to reprint these Edmondsons when it was increased.

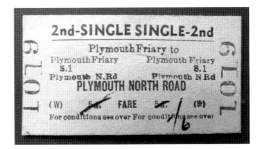

I boarded the train, sitting in solitude for half an hour, watching torrential rain lashing against the platform side of the coach and gushing through gaps in an ill-fitting sliding window. This then trickled in a growing stream down the entire length of the corridor. One other soggy passenger joined us and to dispel the Friary myth we finally lurched off towards North Road, with me heaving a mental sigh of relief.

Once I'd dried out I thought rather fondly of Friary and the whole episode. Sadly, I never did have the opportunity to pay a return visit, so failed to take any photographs of this outpost of Waterloo. What that atmospheric visit undoubtedly did though was to stimulate my interest in all the Southern lines to the west of Exeter.

There are ways and ways of rebuilding things! The marvellously named rebuilt Bulleid light pacific *Westward Ho!* waiting at the newly re-built Plymouth North Road station with a train for Exeter via the Okehampton route. Readers are left to decide for themselves which is the most pleasing.

2

TO ILFRACOMBE EVENTUALLY

A Saturday in June 1959

I was most fortunate to have left full-time education at a time when jobs were very plentiful and having a choice, naturally opted for employment that did not demand any weekend working, leaving me free to pursue my own interests. There was now also what seemed then like a vast increase in my spending power, which meant I could afford to travel further afield. Having said that, the 32 shillings (£1.60) exchanged at Bristol Temple Meads for a return ticket to Ilfracombe did seem quite a lot of money at the time, although the fact that I was issued with a rather fine GWR monthly ticket slightly sugared the pill. Just how this Edmondson ticket had survived unissued for at least eleven years at this busy station remains one of life's little mysteries – surely it was not through a lack of travellers to the North Devon coast.

As the day wore on however, I began to think that maybe the old Great Western still had something of a grudge against that part of the world and anyone foolish enough to think of going there, even though they were using GWR metals for a sizable chunk of the journey. Having started in a promising way things then started to slide rapidly downhill. Maybe I simply misread the timetable but somehow my train seemingly managed to lose over half an hour between Bristol and Taunton, dumping me out beside an empty bay platform where there should have been a connection waiting. Faced with two hours to wait before the next Devon and Somerset Line departure, I calculated that the 'connection' I should have been snugly aboard had probably reached somewhere between Norton Fitzwarren and Milverton by now.

Undaunted, I sought comfort fodder in the depths of my bag and mentally penned letters of irate content to obscure railway officials.

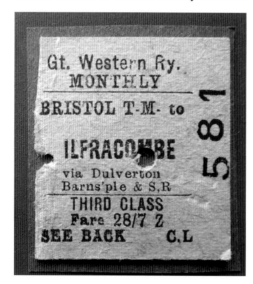

The torn remains of my GWR Monthly Return to Ilfracombe issued in 1959. Despite the clearly printed fare, which was presumably correct in Great Western days, I was charged 32/- or £1/12shillings (£1.60 in today's money.)

Having been caught once, I hardly dared leave the vicinity of the bay platform, hovering near it in case an extra train should magically appear. Of course no such thing happened and it was not until about an hour later that ex-GWR mogul 6337 backed down with the two non-corridor coaches that formed the 10.25 departure. Unlike the 8.30, this train did not run through to Ilfracombe but terminated at Barnstaple; well at least it was going in the right direction.

I hastily bagged a corner seat, which was just as well because long before 10.25 every compartment simulated a sardine tin. Far more people wanted to travel than could possibly be squeezed or shoved in – you could almost hear the old Great Western tut tutting to itself about these misguided souls bound for the wrong resorts. Tut tutting there may have been but summer Saturday or not nobody attempted to find any extra carriages, so some of the unfortunate souls had to pace the platform and hope there would be room on the 12.50. I thought this was an appalling bit of PR on the part of the Taunton staff and could hardly believe that an extra coach couldn't have been persuaded to leave its siding to deal with the overcrowding, there seemed to be plenty sitting around after all. In my opinion the fact that this train was running with non-corridor stock was in itself bad enough, on such a protracted journey.

Forty-five and three-quarter miles, fourteen stops and two non-corridor hours later, after the lengthy reversal at the train's 'proper' (i.e. GWR) destination at Victoria Road, we were all unceremoniously turned out onto the island platform at Barnstaple Junction. At last we were in Southern territory, where signals went up, the dominant colour was green, and tracks were coated in oil from leaking Bulleid pacifics.

Barnstaple Junction, a busy place on occasions but as with most junctions there were long periods of calm followed by bouts of frenetic activity as trains rolled in from various directions. In spite of its three platforms, two signal boxes, extensive goods facilities, engine shed, turntable and coaling stage, the station was never actually that well situated for the capital of North Devon, which lay across the long bridge on the far bank of the River Taw.

Although the North Devon Railway had constructed an imposing stone station building the goods shed, adjoining the up platform, was a wooden structure as was the somewhat dilapidated engine shed. Alongside it however were signs that the original broad gauge shed might have been stone built with an arched doorway. The 50ft turntable here was actually too short for the Bulleid pacifics, which could consequently often be seen clanking around tender first. Ilfracombe's 65ft turntable was able to handle these engines so they sometimes ran light to this end of the line for turning, although how many extra tons of coal per annum were used in this way has probably remained unrecorded.

The passengers from the Taunton train were meanwhile milling around on the island platform and still waiting to travel hopefully

Southern mogul No 31847 arrives at Barnstaple Junction with a semi-fast train from Salisbury in June 1959. The white signal just faintly visible to the left of the tallest pole on the engine's left hand side marks the spot where the GW line from Victoria Road station crosses the River Taw.

– did they really all fit into the 10.25? The coaches had been abandoned at the outer face of the island platform by the Great Western mogul, which had subsequently sneaked into the vicinity of the Southern shed for refreshment. A trio of elderly M7s, already in occupation, didn't seem to raise any objection.

Presently a raised signal at the up end of the station announced the imminent arrival of a semi-fast train from Salisbury. Heads turned, but alas the air of expectation was somewhat spoiled by the appearance of incredibly filthy Southern 2-6-0 No 31847, five exceedingly ill-assorted coaches and a van. At least everybody somehow managed

to get on board and my spirits were raised when the mogul slunk off to the shed to be replaced by streamlined West Country Class pacific *Tamar Valley*, which unknown to us had apparently been lurking out of sight beyond the nearby road bridge over the Torrington line to our left.

We were soon off, swinging away from the Torrington tracks and picking up the tablet for the single line section from the signalman of 'B' box, which was in the V of the junction. This had originally been known as West box and had replaced an extremely tall tower-like signal box that dated from the opening of the line in 1874. 'B' box was unusual in that the signalman had the luxury of a long veranda, constructed in such a way that he could exchange single line tokens with locomotive crews on both lines at cab level, without having to descend to the ground.

The line now curved in a huge reverse 'S' to get us across the River Taw on a long sharply curved, rumbling metal viaduct and along the quayside to the third station, Barnstaple Town. Apart from being most convenient for travellers to the town, this had of course been the interchange station for the narrow gauge Lynton and Barnstaple Railway. Alas there was no Lynton train to meet us today, but although the bay platform was empty, I imagined that the narrow lines still rusted quietly, just out of sight below the

edging stones. Closed some six years after Barnstaple, the country's oldest borough, celebrated its millenary in 1930, the L&B had a short life but is well remembered and will surely flourish again.

After a slipping Bulleid start it was over the River Yeo on a swing bridge before double track was regained at Pottington signal box, then we were steaming along the estuary at a good pace, swinging inland behind the airfield at Chivenor. At Braunton, where the running-in board announced 'Braunton for Saunton Sands and Croyde Bay,' there were the two empty sidings where banking engines would lie in wait ready to assist trains on the stiff climb up to Mortehoe. Although speed slackened as the

loco got to grips with the three miles of 1 in 40 gradient, we apparently needed no help, although the SR mogul maybe couldn't have coped with this train unaided. The fearsome gradients on this line were why Beyer Peacock had supplied the famous Ilfracombe Goods locomotives back in the 1870s.

In spite of the superpower at the front end our speed gradually slowed to a mere walking pace, until at last we panted into the bleak windswept Morthoe & Woolacombe station over 600 feet above sea level and with distant views over Bideford Bay. Putting my head out of the window to watch an up train approaching I realised that the very strong headwinds had hardly helped our progress. There was a small tree beside the up platform, leaning slightly and with its branches growing on one side only, away from the prevailing winds, and this was a good indicator of the normal weather conditions hereabouts! The station looked a bit drab and not exactly a welcoming sight to arriving holiday makers. Both platforms had rather ugly steel canopies which had obviously been added as a modern afterthought, although I doubt they would have kept waiting winter passengers very dry at this exposed location.

Now came some exhilaration as if *Tamar Valley* had suddenly been given her head to rush down the two and a half miles of 1 in 36 to the terminus at Ilfracombe. Had the driver heard of my earlier delays? Was he keen to give me my 32 bob's worth? I didn't check the speed of our descent but it did seem to be hair-raisingly fast by anyone's standards. Through twin bore tunnels we clattered, swaying around the long curve above the Slade Valley that brought the station into sight. Just like a model it looked, perched in

Barnstaple Junction engine shed in the spring of 1960 with an Ivatt 2-6-2T and un-rebuilt Bulleid pacific *Calstock* on view. A GW mogul which had worked through from the Taunton – Barnstaple line can just be glimpsed on the extreme right.

mid-air at that, with nothing behind those buffer stops save space and, eventually … the sea.

I clung to the open window, enjoying the thrill of rushing past the heather at an ever quickening pace. A slight touch of the brakes hardly checked our speed at all. The signal box passed in a blur, the platform rushed to meet us and the brakes jolted full on, bringing us to a grinding, shuddering stop only feet from the buffers … most uncivilised!

The station sat on a sort of man-made plateau 200 feet above sea level. Had I realised earlier that some of the platform itself was on a 1 in 71 gradient and that the 1 in 36 continued right to the beginning of that platform, then my previous excitement might well have turned to terror. Once you studied the place it was easy to forgive the driver his rather crude arrival. Even with the naked eye the terrifying gradients were obvious and finesse with the vacuum brake was undoubtedly not the way to avoid running through the buffers, as the driver of C.M.E. Dugald Drummond's special inspection train apparently found to his cost on one occasion.

The station's superb position commanded a view of town and sea and was flanked by sweeping hills. On one side a substantial stone goods shed dominated the yard and to the other side of the single island platform were seven carriage sidings. From this particular direction howled the prevailing westerly winds and at the buffer stops end the main arrival platform had not only been lengthened, but a large wooden screen and overall roof had been constructed here to prevent any waiting passengers from being blown off the station.

Two Bulleid light pacifics meet as they run into Barnstaple Junction with trains to and from Ilfracombe. The 'B' signal box is just visible to the left of the train entering platform 1, which is the original part of the station. The Torrington line sweeps away to the left beneath the distant road bridge.

Opposite the brick signal box was the single road engine shed, a modern concrete block construction not unlike a bloated DIY garage I thought. The yard area had, by the look of it, been blasted out of the surrounding rocky hillside in order to fit everything in, particularly the turntable. Nevertheless the small yard still appeared woefully inadequate for 3 SR moguls, 2 Bulleid pacifics and one of Mr. Drummond's M7s which were soon joined by another light pacific, bucketing down the bank in a cloud of dust. In such a restricted space engine preparation and movements would have needed careful planning, something the Southern seemed particularly

good at with its penchant for through carriages and the splitting of trains.

Departing trains made painfully heavy weather of the ascent from Ilfracombe to Mortehoe. A Woolwich mogul with three coaches, eventually destined for Waterloo, started manfully up the graded platform but soon lost speed until its exhaust became so slow and laboured that one felt it must surely stall. Somehow it staggered on, finally passing out of sight at least ten minutes later with any unaccustomed passengers no doubt wondering if this was to be the pace of their progress all the way to Waterloo.

While this little drama was being enacted, two coaches and two vans were shunted into

Above: Two elderly Drummond M7 residents at Barnstaple Junction's rather sooty shed in 1959. Sooty and sagging it might be but at least it still retained the roof, which it later lost. On the extreme right can be glimpsed what is possibly remains of the old broad gauge engine shed with what appears to be a bricked-up arched entrance, the building behind being a later wooden addition.

Right: Ilfracombe from near the end of the almost featureless platform with three SR 2-6-0s in residence. Even this end section of the platform was on a 1 in 71 gradient, clearly visible on the right hand edge and beyond the platform this steepened to 1 in 36. The seven carriage sidings on the left could become quite full on busy summer days. Just visible is part of the quite small L shaped station building which greeted passengers who had staggered up from the town below. There was at least a refreshment room and a cup of tea must have been very welcome for those carrying heavy suitcases. The imposing, lengthy goods shed on the right had once been a very busy place in the days before the rise in road transport.

the departure platform and labelled 'Exeter' and I was quite amazed when *Tamar Valley* and sister engine *257 Squadron* both backed down from the shed to haul them. This super power for such a light train was presumably prompted by operating convenience rather than necessity, but the opportunity seemed too good to miss and I was unable to resist the temptation to jump aboard and position myself at an open window in the last coach.

As we galloped off up the platform in fine style and whistled our way past the shed, I glimpsed the turntable and remembered stories of turning the beaver-tail observation car from the all-Pullman *Devon Belle*. On very windy days it would apparently turn so easily that the problem was actually stopping it again. I've heard that on such occasions it was not unknown to throw sleepers into the turntable pit in order to bring the whole thing to a halt!

That same Atlantic wind was blowing with a vengeance now, but it didn't stop the streamlined pacifics speeding up the 1 in 36, a fine sight recorded by my faithful folding Zeiss from the open window. How I would love to have seen the *Devon Belle* attacking the climb through this beautiful valley headed *and* banked by Mr. Bulleid's brand new pacifics.

At Mortehoe & Woolacombe I was

Looking up the 1 in 36 from the end of the platform at Ilfracombe. In the distance is an SR mogul with three coaches which had left the station well over five minutes previously! On the left the crowded engine shed with an M7 and a Bulleid pacific visible. There were in fact no less than seven locomotives actually in occupation.

amazed to find that the carriages were actually rocking in the gale and we rushed down through Braunton to be greeted by heavy rain. At Barnstaple Junction it was farewell to the pacifics as they both set off for Exeter in a tremendous cloudburst. With their whistles wailing mournfully, wheels slipping madly, and that westerly wind whipping steam from the sizzling safety valves down across the puddle filled platforms, they clanked off to be lost in the gathering gloom.

A Great Western mogul drew a train of vintage GWR carriages out of a siding somewhere; it was obviously going my way so I scrambled quickly into a dry corner. I think I was the only passenger and soon we were splashing our way back across the Taw and swinging up round to Victoria Road. The engine crew in the very minimal cab with which these 2-6-0s were fitted must surely have got pretty wet, even with a storm sheet fitted, and were no doubt cursing the weather as they were having to work this section of the journey running tender first.

There were a few passengers about but the business of running round seemed to take an age. Just as I thought we were finally starting, the train hadn't got very far before it ground to a halt and then was shunted ignominiously back into the short bay

Superpower as Bulleid pacifics 34024 *Tamar Valley* and 34072 *257 Squadron* charge up the Slade Valley on the 1 in 36 gradient out of Ilfracombe. Photographed from the rear of the last coach of this two coach & two van train bound for Exeter in 1959.

platform. There followed a long wait, with all the windows steaming up, and we were seemingly forgotten, until eventually the down train arrived from Somerset and cleared the single line. Exchanging tokens meant two excursions into the deluge for the unfortunate signalman before we set off for Taunton in the gathering dusk, rain sweeping down from Exmoor and shot-blasting the carriage windows.

3

PILGRIMAGE TO WADEBRIDGE

Tuesday 18th August 1959

A few days holiday with relatives in Torquay was actually a good excuse for my very first visit to Cornwall. At that time three Beattie well tanks, still stationed at Wadebridge in connection with the Wenfordbridge line, exerted an almost magnetic attraction. These ancient engines, having started life in the 1870s, were the oldest design still running on British Railways at the time. I had seen photographs of them in books and magazines and loved their antique appearance, so a pilgrimage to pay homage before it was too late, plus a short break in South Devon at the same time, seemed a good idea.

A gleaming GW Castle drew me slowly through the rumbling ironwork of Brunel's Saltash masterpiece to that landscape of innumerable inlets and wooded valleys across the Tamar. Noon found me at Bodmin Road station vainly searching for the refreshment room clearly advertised in the timetable. After an exhaustive search however I came to the reluctant conclusion that it had somehow been concealed by delinquent piskies. When a fellow traveller told of its legitimate closure only a week previously I tried to ignore pangs of hunger, putting all thoughts of lunch aside in order to photograph the Bodmin branch train instead. This comprised a 'B' set headed by GW small prairie 5551, into which several barrow loads of mail from the down express were

being thrown with some alacrity by a couple of railwaymen.

Then doors were clapped shut and we were off up the gradient for Bodmin, the loco's crisp bark echoing through surrounding woodlands. 5551 ran around the train at the General station before we skirted around the town, our subsequent progress down the hill to Boscarne Junction being

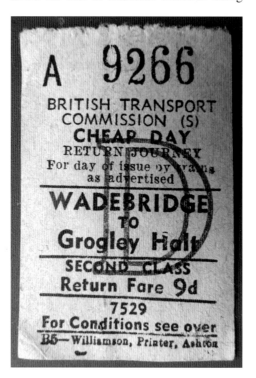

what Charles Rous-Marten might have described as "a hurricane descent". Somehow the section's single line token must have been safely exchanged and we even managed a brief pause at Nanstallon before plunging across the pretty lane to the nearby village and racing on at great speed. Possibly the driver was as anxious about his lunch as I was now beginning to feel about mine, but whatever the reason we sailed majestically past lonely Grogley Halt, before shuddering to a stop which must surely have emptied every loaded forward facing luggage rack in the train. After an ignominious reversal, the guard was able to step out onto the empty platform in order to perform the customary ritual with his green flag before the race once more resumed along this secluded wooded valley of the River Camel.

At Wadebridge, my attention was immediately divided between the somewhat sticky contents of a temperamental chocolate slot machine on the platform and the station pilot, Beattie well tank No 30586. Both were basking in the heat of the midday sun and I'm ashamed to say that at that moment sustenance took precedence over photography as I leaned on the goods yard railings beside the simmering well tank, separating the silver paper from soft warm chocolate.

Porters load mail from a down express into the Wadebridge train at Bodmin Road on a hot summer day in August 1959. My justification for including such an obviously Western Region scene, in a book about the Withered Arm, is that I refer to it in the narrative, although I can never view this photograph without remembering my missed lunch!

Nothing much stirred at Wadebridge, the town and station seemed equally deserted, the oppressive heat probably having driven everyone indoors. The merest movement, a wisp of steam from 30586, seemed to emphasise the stillness around me, although the station cat languidly licked a paw while eyeing me warily. I noted the original Bodmin & Wadebridge Railway engine and carriage sheds just along the line towards Padstow, took photographs and explored the two road wooden engine shed beside the river. This building, unlike its distant cousin at Barnstaple Junction, was very smartly painted. There was a large heavy-duty hoist dominating the tracks in the yard to the front of the shed and I learnt that fairly major work on the locomotives was carried out here, rather than sending them to far away Exmouth Junction. Inside the shed was another well tank which was not in steam. The third 2-4-0WT was presumably pottering around further up the River Camel at Wenfordbridge I assumed, the working of this sinuous goods only line with its

important china clay traffic being the sole reason for these locomotives' long survival here.

Incredibly the Beattie Well Tanks had been at work in the area for some 66 years, the first having braved the treacherous voyage around Lands End whilst being delivered by sea

from Southampton in 1893. The parent London & South Western Railway did not have a physical connection with the Bodmin & Wadebridge Railway until some two years later. The B&WR was actually the first locomotive hauled line in Cornwall, dating from 1834 when it made its money by

Veteran LSWR Beattie well tank 2-4-0WT 30586 on station pilot duties at Wadebridge on a sweltering August day in 1959. On the right are the large water tower and part of the wooden engine shed. The far more substantial B&WR engine shed of 1834 can be seen alongside the Padstow line, to the right of the starter signal on the platform and immediately left of the white buffer stop.

The view from Wadebridge station footbridge looking towards Bodmin. A game of cricket is in progress beside the River Camel on the left and a T9 4-4-0 which has just arrived from Padstow with a train for Bodmin North is about to uncouple and be replaced with an Adams 02. The East signal box can be seen in the distance just before the line curves to the left.

transporting sea sand from the Camel Estuary inland for agricultural purposes. It was acquired, illegally it seems, by the South Western in 1846, when that company's rails were still about 200 miles away, a move that could certainly be termed as forward planning as it took them until 1895 to link up with this far flung outpost of their empire!

We return to Wadebridge on that hot, sticky afternoon in 1959 and 30586, finally rousing itself from its lunchtime siesta, stirred the station into some form of life with a display of spirited shunting. As if this was the signal for a bout of intense activity, loud clanking heralded the arrival of a T9 with a passenger train from Padstow, although the 4-4-0 was quickly uncoupled and replaced with a gleaming Adams 02 0-4-4T from the shed to take the train on to Bodmin North. Another T9, 30338, steamed in with a Padstow – Exeter train and while this locomotive was being exchanged for a Southern mogul

another 2-6-0 arrived with a down North Cornwall line working. To complete the picture a GW small prairie tank with a Bodmin Road train ran in to the remaining platform and there was only just enough room to fit everything into the station!

A flurry of station staff hurried from cool dark corners, and platforms were suddenly bustling with barrows and suitcase lugging passengers. 30586 shunted noisily in the yard, clouds of dust billowed from the shed as coal was heaved into those very long T9 eight-wheeled tenders and the signalman in the grey granite East signal box clattered levers, rang bells and wiped his no doubt sweaty hands on a grubby duster.

My watch told me that it was soon time to start heading back towards Torquay and although it rather vexed me to have to leave Wadebridge in something other than a Southern train, I told myself that I would soon return to explore the whole area further. So 4553 took me back to Bodmin Road and as we passed Boscarne the Wenfordbridge goods train must have been just out of sight, waiting for us to clear the section before it was allowed out through the gate from the branch to waddle back to Wadebridge in time for tea.

Drummond T9 4-4-0 30338 approaches Wadebridge East signal box. In the background every platform at the station is occupied with, left to right, a train for Padstow, a North Cornwall line train headed by an SR mogul and a Bodmin Road train with a GW small prairie tank. The arched bridge over the River Camel can be seen above the buffer stop to the right of the engine.

Wadebridge shed with an unemployed Beattie well tank resting inside. The heavy lifting gear, on its short length of extra-broad gauge track enabled fairly major work to be carried out at this Cornish outpost of the Southern. The turntable is to the rear of the shed and the proximity of the River Camel is indicated by a glimpse of the arched bridge on the right.

9.05am on the station clock and a typical North Cornwall line train arrives at platform 1 Wadebridge behind SR mogul 31840 and comprising Maunsell stock with the usual collection of assorted vans. To the right of the very utilitarian Southern concrete footbridge can be seen the roof of the goods shed.

4

The DARTMOOR LINE

August 1959

Exeter St Davids must have been a very confusing place to the uninitiated when one could stand and watch two trains, both Plymouth bound, depart in completely opposite directions. The Western one scurried along the coast and climbed over the notorious South Devon banks. The Southern train however set off up the Great Western main line towards Taunton but swung off to the left along the erstwhile broad gauge Exeter & Crediton route at Cowley Bridge Junction.

Cheap Day return tickets to Plymouth at 4/6d (22p) were available by either route in 1959 and I remember thinking I'd certainly

had my money's worth following a journey around the fringe of Dartmoor behind a smart 'air-smoothed' Bulleid pacific. A succession of images stayed with me: turning away from the GW main line and crossing the River Exe at Cowley Bridge

into what for me was completely new territory, and the broad gauge style buildings at Crediton contrasting with the very basic wooden structures at Yeoford, the next station. I thought the huddle of clapboarded buildings at this junction station looked somewhat temporary, when compared with the substantial stone water tower and chunky signal box, the latter having an extremely squat weatherboarded top sat on a high stone tower. I'd not seen another LSWR box quite like this and its construction was no doubt to give the signalman a view across the adjacent road bridge which was between him and the station.

The up side former Broad Gauge station building at Crediton pictured in 1964.

We turned away from the North Devon line and soon there came very imposing buildings at the lonely stations of both Bow and North Tawton, with their arched windows and impressive rows of tall chimney stacks. Then we were back with a rather utilitarian little building at the next stop, once the railhead and named Okehampton Road, but then re-named more picturesquely Belstone Corner before officialdom finally settled on Sampford Courtenay. From the window Dartmoor began to dominate the view with the Belstone tors and Yes Tor itself in sight.

Then we were curving to the right over a granite viaduct, running along the crowding slopes of East Hill, past the little engine shed and into Okehampton station, itself clinging to the hillside high up above the town.

I was pleased to see a sizzling T9 waiting

Bulleid light pacific *46 Squadron* entering Exeter St Davids from the Paddington end of the station with a train from Plymouth via the Okehampton line in 1959. The Z class banker waits patiently for the train to stop in the platform before joining at the rear to assist it up the 1 in 37 bank to Exeter Central. The Red Cow Crossing keeper pacing the long roadway must have had an unenviable job during the winter months!

with the North Cornwall line connection on the other side of the platform here. There was the urge to bundle in behind this ageing greyhound and savour that long lonely journey down to the Atlantic coast, but I was expected back at my aunt's in time for tea. So I stayed with the Plymouth train, climbing away from the station as to the left loomed the overpowering mass of the Moor, to the right the West Okement Valley and Okehampton's gaunt ruined castle.

After a glimpse of the little G6 Departmental locomotive shunting in Meldon Quarry, we rumbled slowly onto the spindly, pier-like viaduct, high above the West Okement River. This viaduct is indeed spectacular and, when viewed from a little way off it looks to be almost too flimsy to take the weight of a train. Opened as a single line in 1874 the viaduct was only half the width of the later structure and appeared even more fragile and certainly in grave danger of toppling sideways into the water some 100 feet below! When the line was doubled only five years later another similar structure was built directly alongside, so that what at first glance appears to be one viaduct is in fact two.

At isolated Meldon Junction the North Cornwall line peeled away in a long sweeping curve to those magical places that were still only names on the map to me – Maddaford Moor, Halwill Junction and surely that ultimate of destinations, the Atlantic Coast itself. Another day I told myself, I'll travel it on another day.

My train was now nearing Prewley Moor and the very summit of the entire LSWR system, 950 feet above sea level. Here we were, beneath the great brooding heights of Yes Tor and High Willhays, as over the

A lone passenger waits on the 'down' platform at an almost deserted Okehampton station on a dull overcast day in the summer of 1960. At the far end of the 'up' platform the small engine shed can just be seen to the right of the lofty water tower.

summit we went, now rattling down the 1 in 80 beneath the Sourton Tors. Bridestowe station, a lovely spot, sadly nowhere at all near the village of course but with a mighty avenue of mature beech trees marching away up the road towards the moor. Somewhere in the vastness beyond lay the remains of the old Rattlebrook Peat Railway which climbed for 7 miles across Dartmoor to a peat works 1,000 feet above Bridestowe station and down which horses had hauled wagon loads of peat to a siding here.

Then Lydford, with the great mass of

Black Down sweeping to literally just beyond the boundary fence but no passengers. An awfully impressive backdrop but rather a bleak place to wait for a train maybe, and well over a mile from the straggle of cottages which gave the station its name, some of which which were actually better served by the previous station at Bridestowe!

The South Devon Railway (GWR) was the first to arrive at Lidford, as it was in those days, with its broad gauge line from Plymouth to Launceston and the LSWR had

Three Southern N class moguls at Okehampton shed
in 1960, with the main line disappearing towards
Yeoford and Exeter on the right. Okehampton town
itself is some way down the hill to the left of the 70ft
turntable which, as with the one at Padstow, was
operated by the engine's own vacuum ejector.

naturally tagged its station on alongside. This meant there needed to be everything in duplicate, staff, signal boxes, water towers etc. etc. In the days before the grandly named Plymouth, Devonport and South Western Junction Railway completed the LSWR's link to Plymouth in 1890, all 'narrow' gauge trains had to creep slowly down to the coast using a third metal laid between the single track broad gauge bridge rails, causing some problems with LSWR timekeeping! Common sense eventually prevailed at Lydford when a joint signal box with two lever frames, back to back, was built to straddle the common island platform and this then controlled the whole site. I was pleased to note that a plentiful number of Southern targets hung on both sides of the station and that there was no sign of any Western Region totems, so the Southern had seemingly established itself

Crossing Meldon viaduct with the wooded slopes of the West Okement River over 100ft below and Meldon Quarry ahead. The tiny platform provided for quarry workers is visible just beyond the end of the viaduct. The train comprises 4 'blood & custard' Mk 1 coaches, instead of the more usual SR stock in green, and is hauled by Bulleid pacific *Westward Ho!* in its un-rebuilt condition in 1959.

as the major player hereabouts at any rate.

The GW and SR routes ran parallel for some way and from the window I saw a GW 45XX on a Western passenger train and another hauling a short goods. Being on the Southern however we dallied awhile at attractive Brentor station below the bleak little village of North Brentor where from the platform, on a clear day, you could see the tiny, granite church sitting high atop Brent Tor's rocky perch over a mile away.

Then it was Tavistock where plenty of passengers were waiting at the station, set high above the town. During BR days the station was renamed Tavistock North, the former GWR station some way off on the far side of town becoming Tavistock South. A busy town and a busy station, reflected in its size and the fact that it boasted a refreshment room. Leaving the platform, we immediately crossed a lofty stone arched

Looking towards Okehampton from the footbridge above the SR platforms, with the LSWR two-frame signal box. The GW branch swings to the left of the standard-broad gauge transfer goods shed, with its arched doorways, while the SR line passes behind the shed and beneath the road bridge visible to the right of it.

The large sign on the long approach road.

The GWR side of Lydford station, photographed from the Plymouth end in 1961, and looking towards the high ground of Dartmoor. This was the 'up' end of the station as far as the GWR was concerned, but the 'down' end for the SR!

viaduct which marched over the rooftops of houses and climbed away from the town. Passengers were soon treated to spectacular views across the Tamar Valley as the train approached Bere Alston, or Beer Alston as it had been when the line opened.

This hilltop station with its marvellous panorama also boasted a little Adams 02 tank engine waiting at the outer face of the island platform with the Callington branch mixed train. Once again I wished it were possible for me to jump out and ride on the mixed train to Callington, but there wasn't time and I contented myself with the promise that a return visit would have be made. In the event

Lydford in 1961, a station dominated by the Moor, which appeared to threaten the railway from just beyond the boundary fence. The view across the platforms from the entrance to the GW side of the station. This would be the 'up' end for the SR but the 'down' end for the GW. Note the Southern targets on the lamp posts, even on the WR platforms!

A Southern mogul with a westbound freight approaching Tavistock, the Great Western line from Launceston is in the foreground.

it was not until 1962 that I was able to organise this.

After a fast run past Bere, or Beer, Ferrers we crossed the long curving Tavy Viaduct with its eight rumbling bowstring spans flanked at both banks of the river with a series of stone arches. Then it was alongside the water and we were soon running beneath Brunel's classic Royal Albert bridge at Saltash.

At Devonport another Adams O2 was to be seen playing with trucks. This once magnificent station had graceful canopies and a most imposing main building but had suffered severe bomb damage during the Second World War and was now looking a trifle sad. It had originally been the LSWR terminus for trains arriving via the GWR lines, but when the Plymouth Devonport and South Western Junction Railway line was constructed in 1890 it became a through

46 Squadron has steam to spare as it is seen coasting into Bere Alston with a Plymouth train in 1962.

station and trains then continued to North Road and Friary, their eventual terminus.

Since Friary station had now closed I had to content myself with a North Road arrival. In 1959 this station was being 'improved' and of course it wasn't only the Victorians who, as with their church restorations, sometimes went completely over the top! A huge office block had reared above the platforms and contrasted sharply with the more humble and human structures of the country stations at which we had just called.

Westward Ho! an immaculate and splendidly named 'West Country' pacific with 4 gleaming red and cream coaches whisked me back to Exeter in good time for Torquay teatime at my Aunt and Uncle's. This was a thrilling run, although I do remember being not at all impressed with what I jotted down in my notebook as the locomotive's rather apologetic hooter!

Westward Ho! pauses beneath the footbridge at Bere Alston with a Plymouth bound train, 1962.

Looking across the branch platform at Bere
Alston. The Tamar Valley is on the extreme right
and in the centre can be seen the hazy heights of
Dartmoor and the steam of a train climbing
towards Tavistock, 1962.

5

TAW & TORRIDGE

June 1960

Elsewhere in this book I have written about the possible confusion at Exeter as regards direction of travel and the same might equally have applied to where one actually sat in a train. Passengers in those days were well advised to read the myriad window stickers with some care since trains appeared to be split up at virtually every stop and it was easy to go astray, particularly after dark.

A train might arrive at Exeter Central with portions for Plymouth, Padstow, Bude, Torrington, Ilfracombe and Exmouth plus a restaurant car which would be detached at Exeter in any case. Plymouth and Cornish portions were again split at Okehampton and also sometimes at Halwill, North Devon portions at Barnstaple Junction. The whole lot had to be reassembled on the way back up to Waterloo in quite a feat of organisation. On busy Summer Saturdays it was the norm to see several different trains carrying carriage destination boards bearing the legend *Atlantic Coast Express* and to the uninitiated, getting your family and luggage into the correct train at Waterloo could have been something of a nightmare.

On the Withered Arm, the Dartmoor route to Plymouth would probably have been considered as the more important line, although some would no doubt disagree as the Taw Valley route into North Devon also carried a fair amount of traffic. In chapter two I've described the exciting method of arrival at Ilfracombe and although the Torrington line was a much more sedate affair it is worth recalling a journey there in the summer of 1960.

I had arrived at Barnstaple on the 8.00am Devon & Somerset line train from Taunton and alighted at a rather run down Victoria Road station. After watching the GW mogul run around the train and continue on its way around the triangle to the Junction, I walked down to the Town station and duly paid my respects to the empty Lynton & Barnstaple narrow gauge bay platform as it waited

GW mogul No 6372 runs round my train from Taunton in the shabby WR terminus at Barnstaple Victoria Road in June 1960. The station was closed to passenger traffic shortly after my visit and this avoided the lengthy business of running around, as WR trains then proceeded directly to the SR Junction station.

silently for its line to awake from a long slumber.

Strolling across the ancient arched bridge over the River Taw I saw alongside the much more recent curving railway bridge, which carried the line from Barnstaple Junction to the Town station and on towards Ilfracombe.

This iron bridge was built on a very sharp curve and had a check rail all along its length. Looking at the supporting pillars, I thought that not only did these appear rather flimsy, but to my untutored eye they seemed to be far too widely spaced to support the weight of the structure let alone that of a modern train.

As the bridge had been in daily use since 1874 however, I assumed it was presumably stronger than it appeared!

At the far side of the bridge Barnstaple Junction was the least handy of the three then existing stations to the town itself, but as the fairly gloomy day had now finally decided to

Afternoon activity at Barnstaple Junction. An Ivatt 2-6-2T runs through the station while a wheel tapper waits to attend to the train in the up platform as it patiently awaits a locomotive. On the right is the side wall of the goods shed, which over the years developed a very pronounced lean away from the platform.

The coaling plant at Barnstaple Junction shed, with SR mogul 31836 and an Ivatt 2-6-2T in attendance. On the far side of the yard, seen immediately behind the Ivatt, is A signal box. The loading gauge on the right is positioned above the track leading into the goods shed, which is alongside the passenger platform and behind the camera.

subject North Devon to some sticky misty drizzle, I was glad of the long canopies here so that I could observe operations without getting wet. Operations is perhaps the wrong word as the whole place seemed utterly deserted and I ended up sitting on the island platform feeling a trifle disgruntled and waited for the Torrington train. 30251, an M7, was shunting under the road bridge round beside the river and as this appeared to be the only activity there was ample time to study the layout here. The sooty black engine shed

was ideally situated since anyone on the platforms could see most of what happened to be at home, but today all that was visible were the GW mogul which had brought me from Taunton, *Calstock*, a rather grubby Bulleid pacific and an equally grubby Ivatt 2-6-2T.

At length this air-smoothed (as Mr Bulleid preferred to call his streamlining) locomotive, slipping on the wet greasy rails, clanked from the shed in clouds of steam, found two very elderly coaches, two even older vans and parked them in the platform

with itself at the head running tender first. A porter emerged from somewhere snug and dry for just long enough to paste up a couple of the obligatory Torrington window stickers. Since I was the only passenger and was always in the habit of asking the engine driver where he was going, if there was any doubt, this job was somewhat unnecessary on this particular occasion.

We ambled off alongside the grey and misty estuary. It was damp at Fremington, where the signal box, of typical LSWR wooden

construction, was perched high above the platforms on a tall brick base. This enabled the signalman to enjoy the fine view across the Taw estuary, where you could see trains on the Ilfracombe line. It also allowed him to keep an eye on the quayside sidings, which had played such an important role in the area's development. In fact the first railway in North Devon operated from here in 1848, the horse drawn wagons of the Taw Vale Railway connecting the quay with Barnstaple, where there were no actual port facilities.

At Instow it was decidedly drizzly as we rumbled through a short tunnel, crossed the main Barnstaple – Bideford road on the level and paused at the station with its rather nondescript wooden buildings. We were now beside the estuary of the River Torridge and just across the water on the opposite bank

Above: Barnstaple Junction shed was well positioned for railway photography as this portrait of Drummond M7 30670, taken in 1959 from the station platform, clearly shows. By this time the shed was beginning to show its age and certainly presented a rather careworn appearance. Although the corrugated iron sheeting looks in good condition for some reason the building ended its life completely roofless!

Right: It was impossible to see that Bulleid pacific *Calstock* was in lined green livery, although someone must have wiped a cloth across the cab-side number and BR original lion & wheel crest on the tender. The engine has just arrived at Torrington with a light train from Barnstaple in 1960. To the right is the milk loading facility which generated a worthwhile volume of tanker wagon traffic.

was Appledore. To reach the town by land however meant a journey of some six miles via Bideford Bridge.

It was raining buckets at Bideford itself and here we spent five minutes beside the water as waiting M7 30671 detached one of our vans at the goods station. In the days when this was the railhead of the broad gauge line from Exeter, it had been the passenger terminus. We then spent another five minutes a little further on along the line, idling at the new passenger station, which being adjacent to the old bridge linking the two parts of Bideford, was in a much better position to serve the town than the original terminus.

Calstock hardly needed its air-smoothed casing as it trundled backwards through the rain at a clanking jog and across a long curving iron viaduct above the River Torridge which, still tidal at this point, was now but a tiny trickle of water. Landcross Tunnel brought the train to the site of the sea lock of the old Rolle Canal, which closed in 1871 when the railway was extended from Bideford. The train now actually followed the bed of the canal to bring me to a deserted Torrington station.

"SOUTHERN RAILWAY TORRING-TON STATION", shouted a huge cast concrete sign on the road side of the running-in board so that motorists rushing past would be in no doubt that although the station appeared to be in the middle of nowhere it actually was somewhere. I've seen a photograph of a super old Southern Railway omnibus that used to meet all the trains years ago but of course there was no sign of it by the time of my visit, and no sign of the town either, only the hill up to it. In view of the uncertain weather I decided to stay near the railway.

The Bulleid pacific clanked off back towards Barnstaple and I was left with two hours to spend at Torrington station. At least the rain stopped and the dramatic lighting department provided some bright sunshine to aid my photographic efforts, but a paucity of negatives of the day in my file probably means I was running short of film. I explored what little remained of the narrow gauge Torrington & Marland clay line, the stumps of some stone piers of an otherwise wooden viaduct across the river being a tangible reminder of what had once been a very busy operation. Sadly the narrow gauge was swept away when the standard gauge North Devon & Cornwall Junction Light Railway opened to Halwill in 1925.

The buildings at Torrington were all of substantial stone construction, except for the engine shed, which was undoubtedly a little brother of the sagging wooden structure at Barnstaple Junction. This depot had apparently officially closed some months before my arrival and the building had completely disappeared by the time of my next visit in 1962. Latterly it was home to three Ivatt 2-6-2 tanks that, among other duties, had the task of working the light railway. One of these engines arrived with the single coach train from Halwill Junction at about midday and another then set off with the down goods – one wagon!

I spent some time on the hillside by the viaduct over the river, gazing down the single line as it meandered through the beautiful valley towards Petrockstow and promised myself that I would simply have to return to travel another day. The extremely frugal train service didn't make it very easy to plan a return trip if one's starting point was Bristol however, and it did mean a very early start.

Back at the station there was still a distinct lack of passengers, but I enjoyed the rest of my stay talking to the friendly stationmaster and his booking clerk, who kindly worked out the timings for my return to Bristol via the Southern route to Exeter. This spared me a wait for a WR train at Barnstaple Junction and meant I could relax undisturbed in a through coach from Torrington all the way to Exeter St. Davids.

My train comprised four coaches ranging in age from ancient to modern, we called at all stations, the Bulleid pacific at the front never seemed to be in much of a hurry and I remember my surprise at noting the long stretch of single track on what I had always thought of as a main route. This began at the picturesque station of Umberleigh, although as all nine stations on the line had passing loops maybe this wasn't such a problem. The North Devon Railway had of course been broad gauge until 1877, so the platforms were wide apart, making each station appear quite spacious. They were also very well appointed, with handsome, substantial stone buildings and well tended gardens.

Portsmouth Arms, named after the nearby pub, had been given a smaller but pleasing single storey building with twin gables, while Eggesford had bay windows. Lapford, where there was a large Ambrosia factory, was unusual in that the up and down platforms were staggered and separated by a three arch road bridge.

At Copplestone we regained double track again and our arrival at Exeter was more or less on time, so not only did I catch my connection, but was also entertained by a very impressive display of Bulleid slipping as the engine struggled to find its feet at the foot of the bank up to Central station.

41312 takes water before setting off from Torrington along the North Devon & Cornwall line with a very light goods working of one wagon in 1962. Although the line saw very few passengers, goods traffic in the form of clay from Marland and Meeth and livestock movements could be quite heavy at times.

Midday at Torrington in 1962 and the ND&CJLR passenger train from Halwill Junction has just arrived. In the days before the opening of this light railway, clay traffic had been brought to the station by the 3ft gauge Torrington & Marland Railway, which had terminated at an interchange siding in the yard to the left of the goods shed.

This fine cast concrete sign, facing the roadway at the Halwill end of the station, left nobody in any doubt as to where they were and who was in charge! Although the photograph dates from 1962, and the Southern Railway had ceased to exist for about 14 years, it was pleasing to see that the BR painters had decided not to eradicate the lettering on the top line. They were maybe old SR men themselves!

Bideford takes the wrong line for its home town as it leaves Barnstaple Junction for Ilfracombe, passing B signal box where the signalman is waiting on his veranda to hand over the single line tablet. In the background an Ivatt tank waits on the Torrington tracks.

The instrument from 'B' Box (above). The original enamel plate had been replaced with an ivorine one when the box had been re-named in 1949 – it had been 'WEST'. 'A' Box was at the other end of the station, where the instrument was plated 'Barnstaple Junc B'.

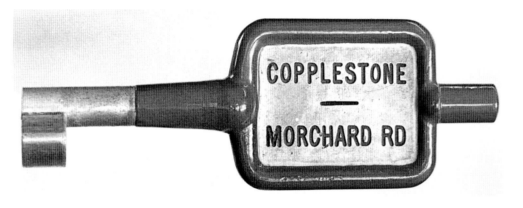

Alloy key token to the Copplestone to Morchard Road section.

6

WAITING AT HALWILL JUNCTION

Saturday 20th August 1960

"There'll only be about three right through to Lanson," complained the guard of the Plym Valley train as he carefully locked up the leading coach, explaining to me that this would avoid having to pull up twice at some halts. I wondered why four non-corridors had been provided in the first place and just where this "Lanson" actually was since I didn't remember it featuring in the timetable. Then the realisation dawned that I was not bound for *Lawn/cess/ton* at all and that for years I had been making an utter fool of myself. The same problem arose years later with nearby Bridestowe (pronounced *Brid/e/stowe* not *Brides/toe*, but that's another story).

The ex-GWR engine shed at Launceston in August 1960. This was still in use at the time, although all passenger trains were now using the Southern station and some WR coaches can be seen parked along the SR line to the right. The LSWR also had an engine shed at Launceston and this was actually opposite the GWR facility, just beyond the right hand edge of the picture.

We were away on time, prairie tank No.5537 steaming smartly out of Plymouth North Road at 10.30am, and I was soon enjoying the scenery as the engine worked up around the southern slopes of Dartmoor. At Horrabridge we passed a similar train while the overall-roofed GWR station at Tavistock produced a well-meaning but misguided porter who incurred the wrath of our guard by unlocking all the doors of the leading coach. A passenger survey would now have shown that those of us who had paid to travel enjoyed the luxury of a carriage apiece.

After plunging beneath the rival SR route high above us we climbed up to parallel it into lonely Lydford's four platforms. No Southern steam in sight but we did meet 4591 and train heading for Plymouth and before we steamed off in the direction of Cornwall I tried to estimate which of its doors might be locked. Our guard was a trifle out in his reckoning for a good handful of people piled out at Launceston, when we drew up at the

Southern station. 5537 sought refreshment at the loco shed and classmate 5572 backed down to return the train to Plymouth, but only after strategic parts of it had once again been put firmly out of bounds to intending passengers.

Apart from some fascinating old streets and a ruined Norman castle on the hill close by, Launceston also boasted a rather fine platform-level signal box. This somehow reminded me of my Uncle Fred's greenhouse, an illusion aided by the fact that in order to explore the now closed GWR station next door, one needed to negotiate the signalman's rose garden. The Great Western platforms were obviously beyond his jurisdiction, being a trifle overgrown. The rival had in fact arrived in the town in 1865, as a broad gauge line, some 21 years before the LSWR appeared on the scene in 1886. Now there were only a few goods wagons standing in the terminus, although the small engine shed was still in daily use.

The arrival of a sooty Southern mogul with an up North Cornwall train cut short my explorations and brought me hurrying back through the thorns to find a small crowd of passengers waiting to board. Off we steamed and at 2.47pm I alighted at that Crewe of the Withered Arm – Halwill Junction.

My old notebook tells of "...a desolate junction in the middle of absolutely nowhere..." I suppose this is a reasonably accurate description of Halwill station and its rather bleak outlook on that particular very dull, overcast and unseasonably chilly day. A minor road crossed the tracks at the up end of the station and from here I was able to watch my train gradually dwindle into the distance as it steamed across the Devonshire uplands towards Okehampton.

The ex-GWR terminus at Launceston in August 1960, looking towards the buffers. This station was closed to passengers in June 1952, after which trains ran into the Southern station on the left. Just visible is the LSWR signal box mentioned in the text and part of the water tower.

There was deep inside me the vague feeling of being a little foolhardy and that maybe it would have been wiser to have stayed snugly on board.

According to the timetable the next up train was due in one and a half hour's time so I had ample opportunity to take stock of my surroundings. The platforms here increased the feeling of bleakness by having no cover whatsoever, buildings were minimal and architecturally somewhat uninspiring after the North Cornwall stations. On the down side the main building with booking office did manage a clock in the wall and there was a very short bay platform with the goods yard and engine turntable beyond it. The up side had a small stone waiting shelter with an empty fireplace and a very lofty LSWR wooden signal box with a good view. An extension, in the same clapboard style, had been added at the Bude end of this box when the light railway to Torrington opened in 1925. A trio of two wheeled barrows looked as if they had lived at the station for many years and one of these carried a number of fresh water containers which were obviously

There is plenty of custom for this 'up' North Cornwall line train, steaming into Launceston behind one of the ubiquitous N class moguls and, although it is 20th August 1960, the clothing worn by most of the waiting passengers gives some indication of the anything but warm weather!

Sporting the *Atlantic Coast Express* headboard, West Country pacific *Chard* arrives at Halwill Junction and the signalman reaches up for the single line token. The later extension to the lofty LSWR signal box, built to house the token apparatus for the ND&CLR, is clearly visible in this August 1960 picture.

dispatched to various railway outposts down the line.

Trains for Torrington used a separate platform at the down end of the station. This had been cut into the bank and was totally devoid of buildings, with no creature comforts for passengers except an overgrown wooden bench. Three tall SR concrete lamp posts and a small wooden sign proclaiming 'Halwill Junction' completed the picture. By way of contrast the concrete running-in boards on the main platforms announced 'Halwill for Beaworthy, Junction for Bude, North Cornwall & Torrington Lines'.

Near the level crossing was a small public house (closed), a huddle of houses named after the station and a road leading off into the hazy distance. Although it was August an exceptionally icy wind was gusting across the station so I huddled in the little stone shelter, consoled myself with a chocolate bar from my bag and wondered what on earth it was like here in the winter.

If Halwill did have any shortcomings in the way of passenger comforts however, it was reputedly a busy place where shunting went on at all hours; "An oasis of activity" was how David St John Thomas referred to it in his Regional History of Britain's Railways. Just as I was beginning to doubt the accuracy of his words things suddenly started to liven up and I certainly did see some intense railway activity, even if I was the only actual passenger on the station.

No less than three standard 2-6-2 tank engines began trying to shunt the dozen or so wagons in the yard – one imagines they were actually taking it in turns. This went on until what I assumed was one of the main events of

the day, the arrival of the down *Atlantic Coast Express* complete with headboard, behind 34033 *Chard*. One loco now had a legitimate job to do since the detached Bude portion needed motive power after the departure of what was left of the main train for Padstow, at something less than express speed.

One of the remaining tank engines, having finally managed to assemble a short goods train, ambled off in the wake of the *ACE*, leaving the third in full possession of the goods yard. The station clock now announced that my sojourn was almost at an end but five minutes before departure time a light engine, in the form of a Southern mogul, sauntered up from the Launceston direction. It ran through the platforms, clanked over the crossing and waited in the goods loop at the Okehampton end of the station until my train, another mogul hauling two rather grimy coaches, a van and a cattle truck, arrived from Bude. Despite the lengthy platform this train strangely ground to a halt right on the level crossing and simmered there for a further five minutes while the first mogul backed down from the goods loop and coupled to the front.

By the time this intriguing combination pulled away, the level crossing gates had been closed to road traffic for approximately 15 minutes, and drivers of some cars and a tractor had given up all hope and turned off their engines. I wondered if this happened every day as we sauntered off at a sedate pace to the next station, Ashbury, where a short but crowded train headed by a Bulleid pacific, its safety valves roaring impatiently, waited to cross with us.

The moguls plodded on to Okehampton

where it was "All change", although to my amazement I was in fact the only passenger. The entire train was parked in the yard and the engines steamed off to the shed, and I couldn't help wondering what happened to those occupants of the cattle truck. I had only a brief wait before the usual light pacific came hustling in from Plymouth with something a little more sprightly than the mixed train, displaying prominent 'WATERLOO' window stickers everywhere.

The only other passengers to join the train were some newlyweds who arrived by car with a photographer and some friends to bid them *bon voyage*. They had to be photographed from every conceivable angle with such superb backgrounds as the water tower, footbridge, up side waiting room etc. before being allowed to board the train. If you were planning to build a model of Okehampton in 1960 then a glance through their wedding album would no doubt prove most valuable! There was plenty of confetti left for the station staff to sweep up, but the train guard was more anxious to get his train away on time than feature in any of the pictures.

The run to Exeter seemed alarmingly fast, so used had I become to the potterings of remoter Devon, and at Central station we were attached to the rear of an up express headed by a 'Merchant Navy' whose pace made even this seem pedestrian. At Yeovil Junction, a nice civilised place with refreshment room, full canopies, covered footbridge and public address, an M7 was waiting to take me round to the Town and a walk to Pen Mill for the 8.27 to Bristol. Halwill Junction seemed a whole world away.

31818, in ashen livery, arrives at Halwill from the North Cornwall line. In the meantime 82025, having pulled its train from Bude out of the platform, waits to attach it to this 'up' working. In the far distance the ND&CLR branch train from Torrington can be seen approaching, determined to join in all this activity. It will pull into its own almost featureless bay platform on the right.

The North Cornwall line train having come to a standstill in the platform at Halwill, blocking the level crossing beyond the platform in the process, 82025 attaches the train from Bude to the rear. To the left of the signal box the steam from an approaching 'down' train is visible. Trackwork proceeds on the right, with the lookout keeping an eye on the imminent arrival. The bay platform is about to be occupied by the Torrington train, which is approaching behind the camera.

The level crossing at the 'up' end of Halwill Junction with an N class 2-6-0 lurking in the goods loop beyond during my visit in August 1960. Motorists who were unfortunate enough to coincide with one of the station's periodic bursts of activity were in need of great patience as the crossing gates would often remain closed to them for considerable periods of time!

7

T9s ON THE ATLANTIC COAST

Monday 22nd August 1960

Bodmin Road station sweltered in noonday sunshine as I joined 5564 and its 'B' set for the climb to Bodmin General, but we had hardly steamed away from the main line before we were engulfed in a torrential cloudburst. Rain drumming on the carriage roof quite drowned the Great Western bark of the engine as it tackled the stiff 1 in 37 gradient and all that could be seen from the window was a wall of water.

An extremely dull damp day at Bodmin General, as described in chapter 7. Attempts to photograph this train from Wadebridge, before it departed for Bodmin Road, were not helped by the all pervading gloom. Although it was August 1960, Cornish summer weather seldom seemed to be as depicted by the publicity departments of the WR and SR, whose skies were always blue!

A brief lull at Bodmin General allowed me to photograph the train before it set off for Wadebridge, then the heavens opened again and sent me running for cover. 4565 with a train for Bodmin Road had been waiting to cross with 5564. There being only one platform, it stood in a siding by the engine shed before backing down into the station after the first train had departed. A porter with a barrowful of parcels to load naturally thought that the driver would bring his train under the canopy but that gentleman had other ideas, stopping it just short. The more irate the porter became, the louder he shouted and the more humorous the driver found the situation but the train still didn't move an inch.

Eventually the rain eased, watery sunshine lit the streaming granite and while waiting passengers made a mad dash for compartments the swearing porter hastily piled parcels in the van. 4565 made a belated departure for Bodmin Road where no doubt all the connections were missed.

It seemed an idyllic summer day again as I walked down into the town towards the towering granite walls of the forbidding jail and the little LSWR station which nestled nearby. Although I was now back on the 'Withered Arm' again, to my dismay GWR pannier tank 4666 was heading the 2.00pm to Padstow instead of the smart little Adams O2 I'd expected. According to the pannier's

SR mogul No 31845 arriving at Bodmin North with a goods train after climbing the final stretch of 1 in 40 past Bodmin Jail, seen on the right, on Monday 22nd August 1960. The washing hanging on the right would probably bear witness to the passing of this engine, which was still working hard at this point!

fireman, who was washing himself in a bucket full of steaming water from the engine, the Adams loco was having the week off. Seeing my disappointment he tried to cheer me, spluttering between mouthfuls of soap, that a goods was due soon and as he spoke an SR mogul 31845 climbed very slowly into view up the 1 in 40 gradient into the station with quite a lengthy train.

The 2pm was fairly well filled by this time and I shared a compartment with a group of local people who obviously all knew one another and no doubt put on something of a performance for the foreigner in the corner. One chap, a fisherman in thigh-high waders, somehow managed to manipulate three rods and a huge basket into the compartment without damaging two middle-aged country ladies with laden shopping baskets, rosy cheeks and straw hats. Opposite me sat an elderly gent in a crumpled suit and after a few nods and winks one of the others asked him the time. This triggered off an act which eventually culminated in the production of a ancient gold pocket watch which had been carefully wrapped in layer upon layer of old newspaper and secreted in some inner pocket.

At Wadebridge the others detrained, leaving me to watch 4666 being relieved by stately Drummond T9 No 30709 and my spirits rose as we clanked off to the blue and gold vistas of the Camel Estuary and the massed fishing nets of Padstow. Here, sister engine 30718 was fussing around with coaching stock and my disappointments of earlier in the afternoon were promptly banished. To see two T9s together was an unexpected bonus.

30709 ran onto the rather exposed, seaside turntable, which on this occasion served as a sort of grubby roundabout when the friendly

Having just brought a North Cornwall line train into Padstow in August 1960, Drummond T9 30709 runs round and heads back through the station on its way to the turntable.

crew gave some holidaymaker's children an unofficial ride round with the engine. There was no pushing and shoving or turning of handles here as this turntable was vacuum operated and even had a tin roof to shelter the operator. As the sides of this structure were completely open to the elements however, I'm not sure the roof alone would have provided much relief on anything other than a very calm day.

I was able to photograph the two veteran locomotives together before 30718 departed for Wadebridge and then 30709 brought the stock for the 3.13pm departure into the single platform. This train comprised two elderly brake end corridor coaches labelled 'Waterloo', a Southern PMV and a 4 wheeled goods van and was apparently known as the 'Perishables'. The driver had a really good oil round his engine since, I was pleased to learn, the T9 was booked to work right through to Exeter, over 87 miles and three hours away.

At Wadebridge one of the ancient Beattie well tanks appeared and attached a rather off-white 4 wheeled van to the rear of our train. Getting rather close to it in order to photograph the proceedings my nose told me that it contained fish! We ambled off up the

T9 30709 on the Padstow turntable beside the Camel Estuary. This turntable was motor powered by the locomotive's vacuum. It not only saved the enginemen a lot of hard work but on this occasion also provided a ride for some holidaymaker's children!

North Cornwall Railway, calling at all stations so that nobody should be denied the privilege of a direct link with the capital. First stop was St Kew Highway, as its named suggests, not exactly handy for the village and then Port Isaac Road, in fact 4 miles from the place of that name.

On departing from the station at Delabole we ran quite closely around the rim of the gigantic hole in the ground that is the huge slate quarry which supplied the North Cornwall Railway with its roofing. Many of the line's stations also had slate hung walls because, although they mostly had substantial stone buildings, the very nature of the line meant they were exposed to the full force of Atlantic gales. Camelford for instance, with its running-in board also listing "for Boscastle & Tintagel" actually sported a canopy, which was unusual on the North Cornwall, and presumably indicated plenty of intending passengers seeking shelter due to the proximity of these popular places. From here there were also views of Rough

T9s 30718 and 30709 at Padstow in August 1960. The driver is giving his engine a good oil-round as soon he will be shunting the stock into the platform for the 3.13pm departure, with 30709 working right through to Exeter. The load of two Waterloo-bound coaches, PMV and van will be considerably increased in number by the time the train reaches South Devon.

Tor and Brown Willy if you looked inland.

From Otterham station, 850 feet above sea level, the Atlantic Ocean itself was visible, but in spite of this fact there was absolutely no shelter provided on the platform. There were few trees to be seen in this sweeping landscape either and one suspects that the GWR would have planted its usual rows of wind-break conifers along the exposed flanks of these Cornish stations, had they been in charge.

Although Tresmeer and Egloskerry were built to the more or less standard company design, red brick had been used instead of stone. I also noted that running-in boards were generally fixed to the walls of the gents, which were built on the end of each main building. In many cases these appeared to be wooden, as were the signalbox names, and it must have been a constant battle to keep paint on all these surfaces.

The signal boxes themselves, with their tall multi-pane windows, would have been somewhat tedious to maintain, given the conditions. Most boxes were on stone bases, some at platform level, some ground standing, and were far more picturesque than the earlier LSWR clapboard design with tiny windows.

Launceston signalbox was of course a sort of double edition since it also controlled the GWR station next door. The important ancient town of Launceston itself, with its Norman castle and narrow streets was just up the hill above the station, but what a hill! Obviously another busy place, it too had an awning, but only a single storey building. Everywhere else on the line had two storey houses for the staff incorporated into the design but the Launceston Stationmaster had a separate house, so that he didn't have to live over the shop.

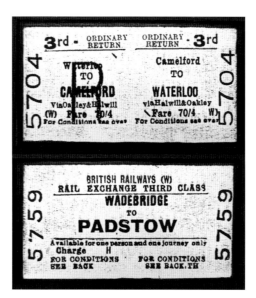

Just south of Launceston we had lurched to such an abrupt halt that I looked out of the window fearing some sort of accident, although what we could have run down in this vast, empty landscape I couldn't begin to imagine. What I saw was about a dozen permanent way men, their day's work done, clambering aboard for a ride home; the PW Wickham trolley was perhaps unknown in these parts?

After Tower Hill and Ashwater we drew into Halwill Junction where an Ivatt 2-6-2T with the single coach Torrington train met us and of course it being Halwill, shunting was called for. Another goods van was attached to our train. Vans now outnumbered coaches, and as they were all different shapes and sizes, made for a rather interesting looking combination. Next it was Ashbury, and then a pause at tiny Maddaford Moor Halt, where I searched in vain for some source of passenger traffic nearby. Soon we were easing round the long curve and crossing

Meldon viaduct to arrive at Okehampton more or less on time in spite of the apparent delays. 62 miles in 2 hours 40 minutes, at an average speed of about 23mph seemed hardly likely to tax a locomotive. Very few people got on or off the train, but station stops were often quite lengthy affairs involving conversations between railwaymen and the T9 had to work hard in between.

According to the timetable only three minutes were allowed here and I was amazed to see that a further supply of 4 wheeled vans was being coupled to the rear, making a total of nine altogether. We now looked, and certainly smelled, more like a goods train than anything else. A note of urgency had now become apparent as we were due in Exeter St Davids, 25 miles away, in about 30 minutes which meant we needed to average over 50mph. This was the moment our driver had been waiting for, the chance to open the throttle and show that Dugald Drummond's T9s were not called 'Greyhounds' for nothing. 30709 rattled up to Exeter in fine style, with speed well into the sixties, screams from the engine's high pitched whistle adding to the excitement of my ride in the leading coach.

That the little fish van stayed on the track was a miracle but it was still there, reeking, when we reached St Davids station and I jumped off to watch the fun as the hefty Z class banker shuffled up behind. The 'Greyhound' sent pigeons fluttering in alarm with a series of ear splitting shrieks, answered by the 0-8-0T at the far end of the station, before both drivers threw their regulators open and the strange cavalcade from Cornwall blasted up the gradient to Central station in an explosive culmination of what had been an exhilarating run.

Beattie well tank 30586, the station pilot, attaching a reeking fish van to the 3.13pm from Padstow during the stop at Wadebridge. The railwayman on the left is carrying a wheel tapper's hammer and one assumes he's checked the little 4 wheeled van prior to an expected high speed run!

Beefy Z class banker 30954 gives a helping hand to T9 30709, at the head of this assortment of stock, as both locomotives charge the incline up around the curve from Exeter St Davids to Central station. The white fish van described in this chapter can be seen to the right of the lamp post.

8

WITH THE GOODS TO WENFORD

Tuesday 14th August 1962

The 1.55am Bristol – Penzance dumped me onto the platform at deserted Plymouth in the grey half-light at 5.15. I walked down through the silent shopping centre in an effort to enliven myself after a sleepless night, but soon returned to North Road where the station had started to stir itself into life. There was a pannier tank with the Tavistock auto, a Bulleid pacific bound for Waterloo, *Kingswear Castle* and a 45XX pottering about. My train for Cornwall stood in the platform, a DMU, so I took advantage of the front seat and ate apples while the driver read his newspaper until departure time at 6.10.

We didn't carry many passengers, mainly BR men going to work, dropping some by the lineside near St Germans where trackwork was in progress. The train terminated at Liskeard before returning to Plymouth, so I had half an hour to wander around and watch another DMU rattle off down the hill towards Moorswater, before continuing to Bodmin Road behind a 'Warship' hauling a Penzance train.

An oily 63XX diesel delivered me to Wadebridge at 8.30, just in time for the local rush hour it seemed. Both town and station were bustling with activity and the two North Cornwall trains I saw were well filled. Just along the line towards Padstow I noted that some of the original Bodmin and Wadebridge buildings were still to be seen, the long

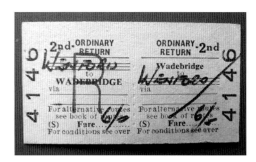

My ticket to ride on the Wenford Goods.

disused 1834 engine shed being clearly visible from the end of the platform. At the LSWR engine shed was a motley selection of moguls, the Beattie well tanks and the three GWR pannier tanks recently sent from the Weymouth Harbour line to replace them.

I was a little disappointed to learn that 1369 was the Wenford engine that day as I had naturally hoped to ride behind a Beattie, but these had performed their last duty on Monday. I was one day too late. The two locomotives still at Wadebridge however were destined for preservation so all was not lost – maybe one day…

I had written to the stationmaster some weeks before in order to arrange this journey and he now greeted me, supervised the issue of a ticket and announced that there were four other passengers for the goods. Another enthusiast, together with his wife and two

sons, was also making this pilgrimage and in view of the crowd it was thought best to add a second brake van. This turned out to be a large Southern Railway eight-wheeler sitting at the back of the yard and the stationmaster came to direct the attachment of this vehicle before we finally set off at 9.30.

The train consisted of 1369, with 5 loaded coal wagons, our brake and the normal 4-wheeler bringing up the rear, swaying along the wooded valley at what was probably the engine's not very high top speed. On the footplate, apart from the crew and the shunter, whose pole was carried across the front of the engine, was the Wadebridge Shedmaster, in traditional trilby and long mackintosh, who had come to check on the performance of the engine as this was a first run.

At Boscarne Junction, where the LSW and GWR lines diverged, we dropped off the 5 wagons – did the signalman use this much coal? We had a long wait here until the following passenger train, bound for Bodmin North, overtook us and we were finally allowed to steam a little way along the LSW line to Dunmere Junction. Here we curved away from the line to Bodmin North and trundled through a wooden gate opened by the guard, onto the Wenfordbridge branch. The gate was then locked behind us and the guard set off on a half-hour walk to return the

Boscarne – Bodmin token to the Boscarne Junction signalman. One imagines that this may have involved the brewing of railway tea, but at length we were away again being flagged across the busy main road to Bodmin at an ungated crossing.

Since leaving the North Cornwall line at Wadebridge we had been running through wooded countryside but now the trees crowded in around us, often meeting overhead to form a tunnel of greenery. 1369 and the two brake vans, more a passenger than a goods train, plodded slowly uphill beside the River Camel and paused awhile in Pencarrow Woods to take water from an ancient tank. I was reliably informed that this tank took its supply from a handy tributary to the Camel and sometimes disgorged fish and various items of rubbish which were not at all desirable to have in the water tanks of locomotives.

Wadebridge yard at 8.30am on 14th August 1962. The Wenford train has already been made up and waits in the centre siding. The train engine 1369, is on the right collecting an extra brake van for the passengers! The mogul on the left is about to set off for Padstow.

1369 waiting to cross the busy main road at Dunmere. Unwary drivers speeding down the long hill from Bodmin might well have been surprised to be confronted with a train trundling slowly across in front of them, protected only by a railwayman with a grubby red flag!

It soon became apparent that the water tank had been built with low Beattie well tanks in mind, they had after all had the monopoly for over sixty years. Getting water into the much higher pannier tanks of 1369 meant arranging for it to run slightly uphill, a difficult task at this somewhat primitive trough. The lengthy stop gave me ample time for photography and alongside the line I discovered one of the original Bodmin & Wadebridge Railway stone mileposts marked in miles, furlongs, chains and yards.

Having satisfied its thirst, 1369 took us on further up the valley to the china clay works with its long row of dries and after half-an-hour shunting we finally drew in to Wenfordbridge itself, some half a mile further on, at about 12.30 – 12 miles and 3 hours out of Wadebridge. For crew and passengers now was the time for the general consumption of sandwiches and, as the sun shone brightly, I went exploring. This did not take long for there were but three sidings and remains of the old incline up to the De Lank quarry, which once exported granite via the Bodmin & Wadebridge. A little country lane could be seen winding its away out of sight and apart from that a small shack, the parcels office, completed the picture. I was afraid to stray too far from the train for fear of being left behind in this peaceful yet remote spot, which was in fact the furthest point from Waterloo ever reached by the LSWR.

The Shedmaster, having finished his lunch, climbed down from the brake van to enjoy the sunshine and we stood beside 1369 while he told me all about his problems with the panniers. He was concerned about the water supply since these GWR engines were very

Was there ever a more idyllic place to stop for water? 1369, on its first run to Wenford, pauses in the sylvan surroundings of Pencarrow Woods, a far cry from its previous life on the Weymouth Harbour line.

thirsty and it was impossible to fill the tanks at Pencarrow. They were also too slow to be used on passenger trains, something which the Beatties enjoyed occasionally. 1369, like all Wadebridge engines, was very clean and there did seem to be some local effort at keeping the locomotives looking good. Talking to the railwayman in charge I could see that there was still plenty of pride in the job at this far flung depot.

Our conversation was cut short by a sudden vicious thunderstorm which sent us scrambling for cover and very soon we were setting off back down to the clay works taking 5 wagons from one of the sidings. After some shunting we were on our way again but didn't get far as one of the workmen came running after the train

Whilst the fireman attempts to coax water into 1369's pannier tanks in Pencarrow Woods, the driver points out something of mechanical interest to the Wadebridge Shedmaster. Being a Southern man he was probably not very impressed with this GWR engine! The round topped stone to the left of the track is one of the original B&W mileposts, marked in miles, furlongs, chains and yards.

waving his arms and shouting to make himself heard in the storm. Apparently we had left the wrong wagons behind and so the guard and the shunter had to venture out into the downpour again, once more unlock the wooden blocks across the private sidings and begin a rather complex shunting manoeuvre.

After they had managed to sort everything out we set off beneath the dripping canopy of branches, rain drumming on the roof in squalls and slashing in on the rear platform where I rode with the Cornish guard. He was very friendly, yarned about his job and told me enough stories to fill a book. As the rain had stopped when we arrived back by the wooden gate at Dunmere, he suggested that I walk up to the nearby halt and ride back to Bodmin North on the 3.25 since to stay on the goods all the way back to Wadebridge might mean missing my connection at Bodmin Road. So, while someone set off for Boscarne Junction Box to retrieve the token, I strolled up the road and found a wicket gate leading down a little rustic path to Dunmere Halt. The whole of this railway system seemed to be hidden away in valleys or screened by trees, it was quite a world apart,

Attempting the impossible, as in order to fill 1369's pannier tanks, water has to be convinced that it must run very slightly uphill from a supply built with Beattie well tanks in mind. Wadebridge's Shedmaster and the driver discuss matters!

A peaceful lunchtime at Wenfordbridge. Hidden away in this remote Cornish backwater it seemed an unlikely place to find a railway terminus. In fact it was the furthest point LSWR rails ever reached from Waterloo, and they described quite a circuitous route in order to finally arrive there!

carrying on daily routines and rituals in defiance of the rushing modern world.

Here at this rural halt, with its pagoda shelter, archaic oil lamps and tiny platform, you might have half expected one of Dugald Drummond's railmotors to steam into view, such was the timeless quality of the place.

The 3.25 was in fact headed by what was known locally as the 'London Midland Tank', No 41272, an Ivatt 2-6-2T which had replaced the old Adams 02 and which carried a plate on its side proclaiming it to be the 7,000th locomotive built at Crewe. It had been given the Wadebridge treatment, was

spotlessly clean and took me back to Bodmin in good time for a stroll across the town to the GWR station and a train for the the main line.

I remember trying to write a letter as we attacked the South Devon banks but sleep got the better of me long before my 9.35pm arrival back at Bristol Temple Meads.

The ex Southern Railway eight wheeled brake van added to the goods specially for the passengers at Wenford. 1369 is gently simmering alongside the normally used van, where the train crew are having their lunch, and the Wadebridge Shedmaster converses with one of the other passengers.

Tight curves and overhanging trees are more reminiscent of a narrow gauge railway rather than a standard gauge branch line. The view from the brake van as the Wenford goods rolls back down to Wadebridge in the rain.

Tucked away at the foot of a path from a wicket gate on the busy main road, Dunmere Halt, with its pagoda shelter and oil lamps has, apart from the photographer, a lone passenger waiting for the 3.25pm Wadebridge – Bodmin North train. 41272, apparently the 7,000th loco built at Crewe, steams up through the cutting from Boscarne Junction.

9

MIXED TRAIN TO CALLINGTON

18th August 1962

In 1959 I passed through Bere Alston on my way to Plymouth, spied the little Adams 02 waiting at the branch platform and vowed to return soon. It was not until 1962 however that I managed to visit the Callington branch by rail and sample the delights of this light railway. After leaving Bristol at 5.45am I was able to make a brief visit to the Fowey branch before returning to Plymouth and boarding a local train bound for Tavistock. At Bere Alston I got off and had over an hour to wait in the sunshine for the 3.15pm mixed train to Callington. Much of my waiting time was spent on the footbridge with its superb views of Dartmoor, the Tamar Valley and Cornwall stretching far away to the west. Trains approaching from Tavistock could be seen miles away as they clung to the high ground south of the moor.

An SR mogul arrived from Plymouth with a short goods train and dropped off a number of wagons before plodding on its way. The branch engine was by now one of the ubiquitous Ivatt 2-6-2Ts, so ubiquitous in fact that I didn't even trouble myself to note its number. It coupled three of the recently arrived wagons to the two coach Callington train which stood in the branch platform. I was disappointed to have missed the 02s which were still working the line when I first passed this way, but tried to cheer myself with the thought that any steam locomotive was better than a diesel and the journey was in any case to prove very interesting.

After Bulleid pacifics had passed with trains in both directions, supplying a handful of passengers, we set off down the 1 in 39 to Calstock at what felt considerably more than the 15 mph speed restriction. There were more marvellous views down into the Tamar Valley before a cutting and an abrupt turn to the left brought us out onto the graceful 12 arch Calstock viaduct, 120 feet above the wooded banks of the river. Although this structure appears to be of dressed stone when viewed from below, it is in fact constructed entirely of concrete blocks which were all cast on site. At Calstock station, on the far side, itself on a very sharp curve to the right, there was a long wait while the engine replenished its water tanks. I was now back in Cornwall again, as the Tamar is the boundary between that county and Devon.

At the Calstock end of this viaduct, when first constructed, there had been a wagon lift which was used to lower mineral wagons to the quayside for transshipment onto river craft. This had replaced a long incline, situated a little way down the quay in the days of the old 3ft 6in gauge East Cornwall Mineral Railway, built from Kelly Bray to Calstock to serve the numerous mines in the area. The ECMR had become part of the Plymouth Devonport & South Western Junction Railway, which extended the line to Bere Alston, converting the narrow gauge section to standard gauge at the same time. The legendary Colonel Stephens, of light railway fame, had a hand in this exercise which must have been carried out with military precision since we are told that the gauge conversion was undertaken

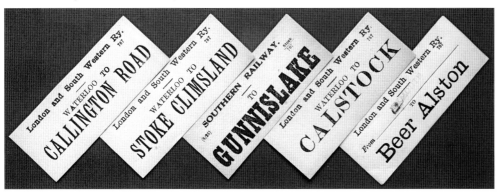

Looking down the line from Bere Alston footbridge, with its superb view across the Tamar Valley and into Cornwall. The main line to Plymouth swings away to the left while the Callington branch train blasts its way up the final stage of the climb from Calstock as it runs into the station.

without interrupting the flow of traffic.

From Calstock the train faced a very stiff climb to Gunnislake, where the gradient of 1 in 38, starting on the sharp curve at the station itself, meant that this had to be tackled from a standing start. There was

much squealing of wheel flanges around the very sharp bends and most of the way to Gunnislake was taken at walking pace with the driver giving long blasts on the hooter at ungated crossings. From the window I glimpsed the main line at Bere Alston, the

view along the Tamar Valley and occasional ruined engine houses from the old mines. I missed the point at which the still discernible course of the original ECMR swung in to join us from the head of the incline down to Calstock Quay however.

At the approach to Gunnislake station we crossed the busy Tavistock – Callington main road on a bridge and there was a respite for the engine as we paused at the island platform. An unusual West Country branch line station in my experience, since passengers gained access to it by means of a short subway which ducked beneath the 'down' line. A fenced path then led to a gate opening onto the 'up' end platform ramp. The corrugated iron building was provided with awnings on both sides and I was rather surprised to see gas lighting here, presumably there was a gasworks nearby but I don't remember seeing any signs of one. As

Bere Alston from the footbridge, looking towards Tavistock in 1962. An SR mogul has arrived from Plymouth with an up freight working and is about to leave some wagons in the goods sidings.

The Ivatt 2-6-2T branch engine, having assembled the Callington mixed train at Bere Alston, prepares to couple up as the guard walks back to collect the tail lamp. An up train on the main line can just be seen departing for Tavistock from the right hand side of the island platform in 1962.

with many rural stations Gunnislake was not actually in the village of that name, which was a few hundred feet down the hill about a mile away. The station itself was actually at Drakewalls, and was on the site of the old ECMR depot of the same name. There was a

good view from here and as a number of passengers left the train I was the sole remaining occupant for the rest of the journey.

After Gunnislake I rode with my head out of the window photographing the marvellous

scenery as we climbed still higher above the Tamar, past Chilsworthy Halt and on to Latchley's single platform with its tin shed waiting shelter, where there was an old ECMR depot and another ungated level crossing. This had been known as Cox's Park in narrow gauge days as Latchley village itself is a good mile away down in the valley at least 500 feet below.

Before Luckett, the next station, we reached the summit of the line, about 700 feet above sea level. From Luckett one could see back to Latchley station and it was also still possible to spy trains on the main line under the shadow of Dartmoor. There was a loop and another ex ECMR depot alongside the station, comprising a house and loading platform. The place had originally been named Monks Corner Depot, and then Stoke Climsland, before settling on Luckett, neither place being anywhere near the station as it happens. Stoke Climsland is at best some 3 miles away and Luckett itself a good mile or so and about 500 feet lower down in the

Ivatt 2-6-2T No 41316 pauses at Gunnislake with a Bere Alston bound Sunday working in 1961. Note the neat corrugated iron building with twin canopies, the subway station entrance and gas lighting.

Luckett in 1961, and 41316 arrives with a Sunday train to Bere Alston, to find at least one waiting passenger. Note the simple light railway design of the station, with its basic seating and fire buckets hanging on the running-in board. Opposite the platform is the former ECMR Monks Corner depot.

valley. Stoke Climsland was at one time tacked onto Callington's name as in "Callington for Stoke Climsland." This is slightly nearer at 2 miles and at least on a direct and reasonable road.

One of the typical cost-conscious light railway features noted at Luckett was the running-in board that also incorporated two rows of hooks for the fire buckets, only one row of which was occupied during my visit! The platform seats here and at Callington were also basic wooden forms and not the usual metal and wood park bench styles of many railway stations. One draws the inference that the good Colonel himself may well have had some influence in these matters.

On leaving Luckett we were soon rattling downhill through moorland, alongside the road, on what certainly appeared to be unfenced track in some places, rounding Kit Hill and entering the terminus, which, by the time of my visit was named just plain Callington. It was in fact a good mile up the hill from Callington itself, in the village of Kelly Bray and had once been called, quite accurately in my opinion, Callington Road. After I had jumped off the train the driver was able to reverse it back along the platform to the run round loop, which was situated by the engine shed, a 2 road wooden affair facing Bere Alston. Not far beyond lay the 1,000ft high Kit Hill with its tall decorative mine chimney dominating the view.

Calstock, Gunnislake and Luckett were all provided with corrugated iron buildings that were pure 'Colonel Stephens' in design. Calstock was shorter in length, while Gunnislake differed from the others because of its island platform situation as already stated. At Callington, although the station building itself seemed identical to the one at Luckett, very close alongside it was a sturdy overall roof which spanned the platform. This was about two coaches in length and, although at first glance it appeared to be an integral part of the station building, was in fact free standing as far as I could see. On a line which was very much a light railway, this doubtless gave some indication of how inclement weather conditions could be at this rather exposed site.

The weather on the day of my visit however, had stayed clear and bright and I was glad to sit in warm sunshine on one of Colonel Stephens' basic little wooden benches, watching the Ivatt shunt the trucks before taking me back to the main line and a slow train to Exeter.

Luckett looking west in 1961. I had arrived at the station with Bob Griffiths and Mark Warburton in Bob's split windscreen Morris Minor, seen on the left of the picture.

A peaceful Sunday at Callington in 1961, with Ivatt 41316 awaiting custom at the station. Note the typical light railway building beside the train shed, the simple platform seat and Exmouth Junction's quite reasonable attempt at a concrete paling fence!

The terminus at Kelly Bray, showing the substantial train shed built hard alongside the corrugated iron station building. The engine of the mixed train is in the process of running around its stock beside the loco shed and Kit Hill dominates these 1962 views.

The signal has been cleared for Ivatt 41316 to
depart with its service for Bere Alston on a
Sunday in 1961.

10

BREAKFAST AT BUDE

Monday 20th August 1962

At 3.38 in the morning the dimly lit platform at Exeter St Davids was chill and uninviting after the close stuffiness of the compartment I'd just left. A mere handful of us alighted and as we walked out past the sleepy-eyed ticket collector the train, my old friend the 1.55 from Bristol, rumbled off into the night on its almost endless amble to Penzance.

Walking through the deserted city streets I saw the odd stray cat, a policeman who regarded me with some suspicion, and not much else. I soon located Queen Street and marched up to Central Station to find much to my disgust that the Southern actually closed down at night. My train was due at 5.10 and at 4.45 the station was still firmly barred and bolted. One or two other hopeful travellers arrived to hang around and eventually we were admitted to pass through the harsh glare of the white tiled booking office and down the concrete steps to the shadowy platforms.

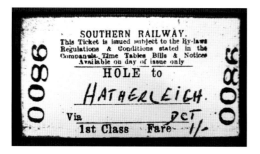

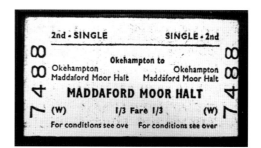

As 5.10 came and went the hopefuls, huddling in pools of ghostly yellow light, began to grow restless. There was much pacing, tapping of feet and consultation of timepieces. One couldn't expect a public address system to start blaring out at this hour so a porter, cigarette end firmly stuck to lower lip, shuffled around the platform cheering us all with mutterings about the habitual late running of this particular train.

From the up direction we then heard the clank of coupling rods and the characteristically hollow beat of a Bulleid pacific announced the arrival of the 1.00am from Waterloo. This proved to be just the sort of thing that one would expect to be trundling around in the small hours. Behind the engine were two centre corridors for Ilfracombe, a few vans, three coaches for Plymouth, more vans, one coach labelled 'Padstow' followed by yet more vans. The 1.00am from Waterloo was the newspaper train.

Getting on board proved no easy matter, for having selected the single Padstow coach as my rightful portion I found the corridor piled with kit bags and each compartment filled with somnolent sailors who did not wish to be disturbed thank you, or words to that effect. Since most of the light bulbs had been removed I stumbled around in the near dark, trudged along the rest of the train and came to the conclusion that a sizeable portion of the British navy was travelling to Devonport that night. It was not until a nice helpful guard went through the Padstow coach and with great courage ordered all the occupants and their kit bags into the Plymouth portion that I then enjoyed the luxury of reclining at ease in a completely empty coach while the navy were no doubt sitting grumpily in the corridors not far away.

While chaos reigned at the rear of the train the leading portion made good its escape for North Devon and we too were soon slipping

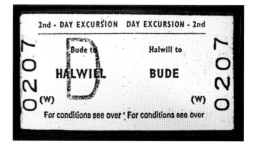

down the incline to St Davids. At Cowley Bridge we swung away from the domain of diesel hydraulics and then like all wise travellers on this part of the Southern at this time in the morning, I slept.

It was raining at Okehampton, a fine drizzling rain that drifted down from the brooding slopes of Dartmoor to blanket the station, high on the hill above the town, in a thick mist. The crowded Plymouth portion slipped off with hardly a whisper leaving the Padstow coach standing at the dripping platform. For over half an hour, there it remained, while a certain softness gently drifted in through the jammed sliding window of my compartment and began to coat me in moisture. Now fully awake, I was just contemplating choosing another compartment when a grimy mogul stirred from the tiny, ashen engine shed and decided that it was time for the newspapers to continue their interminable amble in the general direction of Padstow.

So we went down past Meldon and swung away from the Plymouth line on the great single track curve across Maddaford Moor. There were no passengers waiting at the

Bude station, more or less deserted at 7.49am as 82025 runs around the train from Halwill. The fine LSWR building here was very similar in style to that at Swanage and was apparently built on the outskirts of the town, in a rather exposed position, in order to satisfy the good people of nearby Stratton, which had been by-passed. Not far away to the left is the Atlantic Ocean and the angle of the trees gives some indication of the direction and force of the prevailing wind!

rainswept halt so we set off again at a very sedate pace, 31823, one coach, one van and an old goods truck. By the time we reached Halwill Junction it was almost 7.00, the rain was lashing the exposed platforms with vigour and I was amazed to note that we were actually running to time. (2 hours from Exeter!)

82025 and two rather down-at-heel coaches in the bay did little to brighten the spirits of one who had been travelling all night but they were labelled 'Bude' and a swift dash through the torrents soon saw me aboard. There was a fifteen minute wait while a bit of unenthusiastic parcel unloading took place and the Halwill papers were unceremoniously dumped on the platform. One couldn't help noticing that they seemed to be sitting in the wettest part and a large puddle gradually disappeared as the bundle slowly soaked it up. The Padstow papers still rode in the van and would of course remain dry for many hours yet.

The few unfortunates in the Padstow train were no doubt dismayed to see their engine uncoupled in order to clank off to the yard. It being Halwill Junction, shunting was obligatory and as we pulled out the mogul had located some elderly coaches to add to its train. I assumed that these were empty stock but I suppose there was always the chance that they were the Padstow portion of some train from the previous day, abandoned and forgotten for the night, spotted by chance by the eagle-eyed driver. To this day I often wonder what happened to those Halwill newspapers.

We continued along what had been the original 1879 line from Okehampton to Holsworthy. The first section of the North Cornwall Railway to Launceston branched to the left and was a later development of 1886. As with North Devon, all these railways arrived rather late in the day and the area's development suffered as a result. I was reminded of one of Thomas Hardy's characters in his novel A Pair of Blue Eyes who, when the lines were being built in the 1880s, preferred to travel from Bristol to Boscastle by steamer rather than trust himself to the tender mercies of the railway, "...*the time saved by speed on the railway being wasted at junctions, and in following a devious course.*" My thinking at the time was that maybe things hadn't changed all that much by 1962!

Bude, 7.49, just in time for breakfast in the station refreshment room which sold groceries, beer, ice cream and cups of tea with biscuits plus any amount of other things across a marble-topped counter. I was joined by the local postman, a bus crew, the stationmaster and some porters, who all came in for what was obviously their regular breakfast, alas I was the only actual passenger.

The railway had not finally arrived in Bude until 1898, as an extension of the line from Holsworthy. The buildings here were all in red brick, the handsome station building had stone mullioned windows, decorative ridge tiles, shaped chimney stacks and a dormer window in the slate roof. A generous canopy spanned the main platform but didn't reach as far as the short bay. The tall brick water tower had lost its curved roof and only the skeletal supports remained, while the companion single road engine shed led through to a turntable, beyond which was the gasworks.

The rain stopped, the sun shone beautifully and so I strode along the towpath of the old canal to stand and survey the Atlantic rollers pounding into the bay. Using wheeled tub boats and inclined planes with rails, the Bude Canal had once carried sea sand inland for use as an agricultural fertiliser. Standing by the sea lock I now had the whole place to myself and at this moment felt that it really had been worth getting up at 1.00am in order to breath some truly fresh Atlantic air.

I returned to the station to find that 82025 had backed a train into the bay platform and at 9.30 it now took me back to Halwill where two typical North Cornwall trains, mostly vans with an odd coach here and there, crossed with one another. The carriages from the Bude train were, with all due ceremony, coupled to the rear of the up working, which would no doubt be coupled to something else before it reached Exeter, let alone Waterloo.

With the departure of both trains the platforms returned to their customary emptiness, apart from the Torrington bay where a rather tired looking Ivatt 2-6-2 tank with a tall chimney and a single Maunsell brake corridor coach had slipped quietly in from North Devon.

The North Devon & Cornwall Junction Light Railway, which opened in 1925, was the last standard gauge line to be built in the West. One really wonders at the wisdom of constructing this railway at a time when road transport was already well in the ascendancy and I'm not alone in wondering why the line was taken to Halwill. Connecting Hatherleigh with Okehampton would have seemed a more obvious route and might have proved far more successful because, apart from some lovely scenery, there is little else in the sparsely populated area traversed by the line. Although there was important clay traffic from Marland and Meeth, by the 1920s it must have been quite obvious that this kind of rural railway would find it extremely difficult

An SR mogul waits at the head of a train in the bay platform at Bude. Behind the carriage roofs is the goods shed, while on the right the through engine shed leads onto a turntable. Near the gasworks beyond, a branch forked off to the right and continued across the open ground to the Bude canal, crossing a bridge over the River Neet before joining the towpath. It connected with a tramway from the beach, up which sea sand was transported to be taken inland for agricultural use.

to pay its way, let alone make a profit. Having said all that I'm certainly glad that the line was built, because for those of us lucky enough to travel on this steeply graded light railway the journey was an experience to be enjoyed and well remembered.

There were two passenger trains and a goods each day and the journey time for the 20 miles was about one and a half hours, not the way to travel unless you had plenty of time to spare or simply no other means of getting about. In fact of all the branch lines I've travelled on I don't think any has evoked such a feeling of timelessness as this one. For the train crew and staff at stations the clock certainly appeared not to exist, although the schedules were so slow that one would probably have needed to go backwards to actually lose time.

There seemed time in plenty anyway for long pauses at all the stopping places, which were often where the line crossed a road or lane going in the general direction of the place the station purported to serve. Hole for instance was some 4 miles away and actually nearer Dunsland Cross station on the Halwill – Bude line! The station was certainly way off the beaten track and really did appear to be in the middle of nowhere, with not even a proper road to it.

Hatherleigh was similarly a long 2 miles from the village, which also boasted the largest population on the line. Its situation was indeed picturesque but certainly would not have encouraged much in the way of local passenger traffic. The situation of the third station at Petrockstow was little different since in this case it was built at the ungated level crossing of a road heading in the direction of the village about a mile away.

All three stations apparently saw plenty of freight traffic such as timber and cattle, as well as that originating from the clay works. Each was a passing place with two platforms, ground frames and the electric tablet instruments in the booking office. The small rather attractive stone buildings, of typical

82025, having just arrived at Halwill Junction with a train from Bude, has run around and pulled the stock back out of the station (centre) to await the arrival of a North Cornwall train, to which it will attach its through carriages. In the meantime on the right, the ND&CLR single coach train from Torrington is seen pulling into the rather bare and inhospitable bay platform.

light railway design, had small canopies which were forward extensions of the roofs, supported by wooden uprights on the platforms. The other stopping places at Meeth, Dunsbear, Yarde and Watergate were much more basic. Although the first two had basic waiting shelters both Yarde and Watergate were simple SR prefabricated cast concrete platform structures with name and notice boards and a couple of posts on which to hang the oil lamps.

At Hatherleigh the station attendant came out to meet the train wearing waders, he'd evidently been fishing. He found someone aboard the train whom he knew and there followed a long conversation while the engine took water, but then it was discovered that he'd forgotten to put the kettle on and the poor guard was pacing the platform waiting for what was obviously his daily cuppa. The pair retired to the dim interior of the station building and the handful of passengers could only sit and wait while the kettle boiled, the teapot was warmed and the water thrown out

A lone passenger just off a down North Cornwall train walks along the otherwise empty bay platform at Halwill Junction before joining the Torrington train, as 31875 continues its long journey towards Launceston, Wadebridge and the Atlantic Coast. Changing trains at Halwill could mean a lengthy trudge along uncovered windswept platforms but on this occasion the sun is shining!

onto the track. Then could be heard through the open carriage windows the chink of china and the stirring of spoons and if the porter had come out offering tea at ten shillings a cup he would probably have had some takers. As it was we just had a thirsty wait in the sunshine and the engine crew reclined on the platform beside the rose bushes. At length the guard appeared with a satisfied smile on his face to swish the dregs from his cup onto the track, "Okay Jarge," to the driver and we were on our way again.

There were lots of ungated crossings, in fact it being a light railway, none of them *did* have gates and this gave our driver an excellent opportunity to prove to his passengers that some LMS engines have a whistle which can make a sound other than that of a wet splutter. After the first few crossings I saw that things followed a definite pattern. We would be bowling along at about 15 mph when on would come the brakes and speed would be reduced to a very slow walk. At about 50 yards from the

The peace and tranquility of a light railway station. Hatherleigh basks in warm summer sunshine in this view towards Halwill. There is no sign of human habitation anywhere and the village is a long 2 miles away far beyond the trees on the left. The attractive station building, like those at Hole and Petrockstow, contained the single line token apparatus and definitely has the Colonel Stephens touch!

Above: Approaching Watergate Halt, just visible beyond the ungated level crossing, with the engine whistling furiously and three other interested passengers admiring the view. Although I was the only person with a camera, I rather got the impression that the others were travelling more for pleasure than business and that without the four of us the train would undoubtedly have been empty by this stage of the journey.

Right: Looking back from Watergate Halt across the ungated level crossing, with its cattle grids and road signs proclaiming that "trains cross here", an idyllic setting which just cried out to be photographed. There had been a siding, facing Halwill and just to the right of the line beyond the crossing, but this had been lifted by the time of my visit.

crossing someone would presumably hang the coal shovel on the whistle chain and leave it there until the tail lamp was way past the road or lane. The whistle made some quite interesting noises, none of which were exactly what one would expect from a steam locomotive but they did seem to have the desired effect of ensuring that we didn't meet any road vehicles. The one car that we did see on the entire journey had stopped some way from the railway and the occupants had got out to admire the view, but the driver made absolutely sure by giving them 3 ten-second blasts on the hooter.

Petrockstow seemed to be in the charge of a large black cat which basked sleepily in the sun between the waiting room wall and the railwayman's bicycle. It surveyed our arrival with disdain before returning to disturbed slumber. I do not recollect ever seeing the chap who was presumably manning the station.

At about midday, after a brief pause at Watergate Halt, we threaded through a deep wooded valley, ran over a viaduct, then under the hill from Torrington and came to rest in the station. Incredibly we were on time, something that I found surprising after what appeared to be our snail's pace progress. There was 10 minutes to spare before my connection took me off in the direction of Exeter again to complete what had been an unforgettable circular tour.

POSTSCRIPT

I was married in 1963, the year that the Western Region took control of the Withered Arm. There followed a change of job, the purchase of a house and the birth of our son. Railways took something of a back seat for a number of years but of course the interest and memories remained, backed up by some photographic negatives in my files.

Tucked away in a box somewhere I also have a luggage label from most of the Withered Arm stations, thanks to the helpful staff at Collectors' Corner at Euston. Edmondson tickets, on the other hand, are not so plentiful since many intermediate stations generated such little traffic. An interesting book is the station inventory from Tower Hill, a small, much thumbed, LSWR notebook first issued in 1912 and detailing furniture and equipment such as signs, barrows, oil drums, lamps, clocks and coal buckets there until closure.

A set of wooden, booking office cash bowls which my wife Ginny took a fancy to at an auction and for which she was the only bidder, were signed, mostly in old copperplate handwriting, by the staff. When we got them home under a magnifying glass we discovered to our delight that they came from *"Bow, North Devon"* and that the signatures ran from April 1888 to 1964. This habit of marking and dating everything applied at many stations of course, including nearby North Tawton where one of the staff stamped *North Tawton 11-2-88* inside the wooden box of type for the ticket dating press. The characterful state of this box, complete with Edmondson's patent plate in brass on the lid, leaves one in no doubt that

the 88 is 1888! The longevity of many such items is incredible, viewed from today's throw-away age, for even if few tickets were actually sold at North Tawton the dater type would have been changed daily and the box must have been in constant use for nearly 80 years.

In the spring of 1976, en route for Cornwall by car, we delivered something to a remote farm at Sheepwash near Hatherleigh. Trying to find our way back to the A30 we became quite confused on the tiny Devonshire lanes that appeared to be taking us round in a circle and I pulled up at a minor

Some examples of Withered Arm luggage labels. The LSWR standard design, bottom centre, was later followed by the Southern Railway also by British Railways Southern Region, The British Transport Commission and even by British Railways (Western Region). The South Devon Railway example shows the old spelling for what we now know as Lydford. What is fascinating about all of these relics of the past, when passengers entrusted a huge volume of luggage and parcels to the railways, is the the incredibly varied selection of quite decorative fonts used by the printers.

junction to study the map. Glancing across the road I saw what was unmistakably some weatherbeaten Southern concrete fencing and beyond it a long, shabby and singularly uninspiring abandoned building. Sighing with relief I now knew immediately just where we were – Halwill Junction! The motor car has destroyed Halwill's isolation and the huge growth in road transport could do nothing but signal the end of the railway routes for which it formed the hub. If Thomas Hardy complained of the slow journey times to Boscastle in the 1800s however, one could maybe assume that the writing had been on the wall for a very long time! Nevertheless the system provided employment for many and vital transport links for businesses and people in the days before personal transport became so widespread.

A few limbs of the old system still cling tenuously to life, visually far more withered than during the days of my narrative. The once important Barnstaple Junction has now virtually been reduced to the status of a halt at the end of something akin to a long siding from Exeter. The narrow gauge Lynton & Barnstaple Railway however, re-awakened from its slumbers, appears to be promised an exciting future and after a gap of over 50 years, I once again rode behind a T9 and even a Beattie well tank to Boscarne Junction on the Bodmin and Wenford Railway.

Diesel units climb from Plymouth to Bere Alston, then struggle their way up to Gunnislake's new 'bus stop' station on the truncated and weed-strewn Callington branch. At the time of writing there is yet again talk of re-opening the line on from Bere Alston to Tavistock. This and the rest of the Dartmoor line should never have been closed in the first place of course, as it

Not quite the Withered Arm but almost! Elderly M7 No 30669 entering the yard at Exeter Central with a single wagon freight working. Photographed in 1959 with the Zeiss folding camera mentioned in the text.

provided a valuable alternative to the troublesome GW seaside route to Plymouth and Cornwall. Subsequent events have repeatedly proved the rank stupidity of this closure, but as with the despoiling of the SR Salisbury to Exeter main line, I don't doubt that old inter-regional rivalries played a major role in this.

The Dartmoor line from Yeoford now goes no further than the quarry at Meldon but the abandoned Okehampton station, on the hillside above the town, has been well restored. From high on the tors one can still look down on the spindly viaduct at Meldon and make out the course of that great sweeping curve away from the junction towards Halwill.

In 1989 Ginny and I paused at Halwill Junction on our way to stay at Dunmere in order to walk the old Bodmin & Wadebridge trackbed to Padstow. The council had provided a seat near to where the level crossing had been so we had a picnic breakfast while gazing along the abandoned earthworks towards distant Dartmoor. A builder was gradually covering the old yard and station site with houses and at that time only the up platform remained more or less intact. We wandered along it past the site of the signal box and brushing through some long grass found the spot where the main platform led round to the bay for the light railway to Torrington. One of the ancient LSWR engineering bricks that formed the main platform edging here was loose and so I rescued it from the bulldozer and brought it home; if it could but talk it would doubtless tell a tale or two.

Photographic Notes

The photographs in this book undoubtedly fall some way short of covering the whole of the 'Withered Arm' area in that certain important locations are either under represented or do not feature at all. Whilst it would have been possible to use other photographers' material to fill these gaps, it has been decided not to do this as the book is a very personal record and simply reflects my own particular interests and even the actual camera I was carrying at the time. Another factor was that, having no transport of my own in those days, the great majority of the photographs were taken while I was actually travelling on the journeys described and thus it was not always possible to choose the best times or locations, although some were taken on subsequent visits. In any case I am not attempting to present a detailed pictorial volume of the whole Southern system as this has already been done perfectly adequately elsewhere.

Those who have grown up in the computer age, where it seems that almost everyone now has a mobile phone capable of taking reasonably acceptable photographs, will find it difficult to comprehend how different it was 60 years ago. Many people's family cameras often only came out of their canvas cases during the annual holiday and my first photographs were taken on one of the then ubiquitous Kodak Box Brownies. This particular battered old 1930s camera was borrowed from my Aunt during the school summer holidays and that very first 8 shot film gave me the photo bug for life. It featured trains naturally, but also aircraft at Bristol Airport where in those pre 'health and safety' days I was able to wander unchallenged all around the tarmac apron in order to photograph an Aer Lingus Dakota which was about to depart!

The first camera I actually owned was a present from my parents and came from Boots the chemists, while my first shot featured a lovely Adams 02 on Ryde Pier in 1956. It was a smart looking little camera, but sadly the lens was of such poor quality that it might well have been fashioned from the bottom of a milk bottle. It accompanied me on my trip to Plymouth Friary but, for reasons explained elsewhere, didn't even come out of my bag that day. Later in 1958 I raided my Post Office savings account and bought a Zeiss folding camera which took 8 pin-sharp images on 120 size film. This was also the time of starting over 40 years of home film and print processing, but that's another story!

The splendid Zeiss came to Wadebridge on my first trip into Cornwall and travelled with me to Ilfracombe. It also produced a number of other photographs in this book, and if it ever had feelings, was probably terrified as I leaned far out of the window with it high above the West Okement River as we

Ballast for the Southern system. An 8-wagon train from Meldon Quarry has just struggled up the gradient from Exeter St Davids and into Central station. At the head of this ensemble is a Standard 2-6-2T ahead of an SR mogul, while bringing up the rear are two Z class 0-8-0Ts. A video of this working would have made spectacular viewing, but such equipment simply didn't exist in 1960!

rumbled across Meldon Viaduct. As there were only 8 exposures on any one film, and money was rather limited, I had to try to make every shot count of course and this explains the paucity of photographs at some locations as I was always in danger of running out of film!

Although the Zeiss was in many ways an excellent camera for railway photography, it lacked a high enough top shutter speed to cope with anything more than very slow moving trains, so I 'traded up' to what I thought might be the answer. This was a Microcord twin lens reflex, of the type much beloved by most press, fashion and wedding photographers of the day, but which I found difficult to use for railway work. It recorded Halwill Junction and the T9s at Padstow, since I lugged this bulky camera all around the West Country during 1960. I was never really happy with it however and the final straw came when I inadvertently double-exposed what promised to be a lovely shot of double headed T9s leaving Plymouth. To say I was not happy is a gross understatement, but this was always a potential danger with that particular camera as it was all too easy to forget to wind on the previous frame in the heat of the moment! There soon followed a change to a new 35mm Yashica rangefinder, the type of camera I've favoured ever since for railway photography.

With 36 exposures to play with one was less likely to run short of film but alas, the Yashica itself didn't last very long as I fell into a deep ditch while photographing trains on the Somerset and Dorset line and wrecked both it and an ankle! At long last however fortune smiled on me and I managed to obtain

A.C.E. destination! The sea-lock gates of the Bude Canal stand guard over a deserted breakfast time beach on 20th August 1962, while the ocean that gave its name to a famous train sends rollers crashing into the bay.

a much used, but very well made and reliable, Aires 35mm rangefinder at a just-affordable price. This Japanese copy of a German Leica M2, a camera which I could only aspire to until much later in life, became my constant companion on railway jaunts for a good many years. It travelled all over the West Country and Wales with me and produced the bulk of my 1960s railway photographs.

The cameras mentioned, like most of their contemporaries, were all fairly simple mechanical pieces of equipment that gave control over shutter speed, aperture and focus. The rangefinder gave you focus but you either hazarded a guess at the strength of the light for the other settings or like me, brandished a separate hand-held light meter to assist you. The lenses were of a fixed focal length so there was no zooming-in on a distant subject, you walked closer to it, or walked further away if you wanted a wider angle shot. This could be quite challenging in many railway photography situations, but most enthusiasts seemed to cope well enough and often produced excellent results! In those days photography was a much more straightforward business than it seems to be today. The myriad settings and adjustments built into some of today's complex digital cameras often get in the way of spontaneity and in any case don't help in the least if you have no creative eye for a picture in the first place!

Finally a word about the actual picture content itself. Some railway photographers concentrate all their efforts on producing what one might call a 'standard' three-quarter front view of a locomotive and train. This is sometimes almost completely devoid of background and might therefore be taken absolutely anywhere as far as the viewer is concerned, since little if any of the location is visible. This is fine if your interest is only in locomotives but falls short of the mark as far as I am concerned. I have usually tried to portray the whole scene, with the train if there is one, being merely the finishing touch to an overall view of any given location. This certainly may not please everyone but for me a more general view of the railway and its surroundings is what I have always attempted to record and hope that this will be appreciated by readers.

ACKNOWLEDGEMENTS

Memories of the Withered Arm was first produced in 1994 as a self-published 32 page booklet which Ginny and I printed on our photocopier. It was illustrated with some of my line drawings and although we originally thought to produce only a hundred copies or so, in the event over 1,000 were sold!

George Mumford encouraged me to re-visit my 1994 manuscript with a view to producing a new version of the book illustrated with some of my photographs. He scanned the pages of an old copy so that the original text could be amended on my current computer, and thus spared me the otherwise daunting two-fingered task of retyping the whole book from scratch.

Thanks are also due to Simon Castens for his friendship, encouragement, dogged determination that this book should be published, and for tolerating at least some of my literary and artistic idiosyncrasies!

My wife Ginny has, as always, been a constant source of help and support. Her eagle-eyed proof reading should have ensured a lack of errors, but if any have crept in they are probably as a result of my own typing inefficiencies.

The author, with the Zeiss folding camera mentioned in the text, in front of the Bath Road engine shed adjacent to Bristol Temple Meads station on a damp overcast day in 1959. *Photograph by Bev Jarman*

FURTHER READING

I hope this book might generate further interest in the old SR lines to the west of Exeter and anyone wishing to explore their particular charm might like to seek out *The Withered Arm* by T.W.E.Roche, originally published by Forge Books in 1967. For a detailed historical account of the system I would suggest studying the Irwell Press series of books by George Reeve and John Nicholas, including *The Okehampton Line*, *The North Cornwall Railway* and *The North Devon Line*. An extremely detailed description by Neil Parkhouse of the building of Calstock viaduct includes many fascinating contemporary photographs and appeared in *Archive* magazine Issue 2.